My Well-Spent Youth

Also by David L. Goodrich

Horatio Alger Is Alive and Well and Living in America: Success Stories of the Under-Thirty Generation

Art Fakes in America: The Lively Business of Making, Buying, and Selling Fraudulent Art from Colonial Times to the Present, with Advice on Avoiding Swindles

The Real Nick and Nora: Frances Goodrich and Albert Hackett, Writers of Stage and Screen Classics

Paint Me A Million
(novel)

My Well-Spent Youth

A Lucky Man's 1930 – 1960
New York-to-Paris
Memoir

DAVID L. GOODRICH

THE Beckham
PUBLICATIONS GROUP, INC.
Silver Spring

Published in the United States by
Beckham Publications Group, Inc.
P.O. Box 4066, Silver Spring, MD 20914

ISBN: 978-0-9823876-5-8

2009925190

Again, for Patty

How these curiosities would be quite forgott, did not such idle fellowes as I am putt them downe!

—*Brief Lives,*
by John Aubrey (1626-1693)

CONTENTS

INTRODUCTION

You've never heard of me.

Unlike most authors of today's memoirs, I'm not a self-aggrandizing celebrity, or a victim of childhood sexual abuse, or a reformed drug addict, or a Promulgator of Profundities.

So why do I think you'll like this book?

I had the great good luck to spend my first three decades—the rich, historic thirties, forties, and fifties—in a world of opportunity and stimulation; I was surrounded by people who were unconventional, talented, and progressive—and who loved me; I was privileged to live and learn in colorful, exciting places, and to know some world-famous achievers, whose names you'll recognize. I see this book as a necklace: my first thirty years is the thread, and stories are strung along it. I've tried to make the stories entertaining—and I've tried to catch the flavor of a unique era. This is partly a "coming of age" tale: how a fortunate child related to his remarkable surroundings, and tried to become a writer, and—for better or worse—his own man.

The most important luck you can have is family luck. The first people you'll meet here are my kinfolk, and I promise you won't be disappointed. Many of them were writers, and that had a strong influence on me. I'm not that visible in the beginning chapters, while the focus is on my family, but thereafter I'm stage center in chapters that cover joyous summers in a unique seaside village ... New York's most progressive grade school during its boisterous infancy ... An old-fashioned boys' boarding school, where a teacher publishes a devastating novel ... A great university; wonderful knowledge and stupid prejudice ... The editorial department of a major book-publishing company in its bestseller heyday ... "Psychological Warfare, more psycho than logical" ... A cheesy/classy, huntin'-adventurin' men's magazine...

And then—hallelujah!—Paris, 1959-1960. For the first time, after living always "by the rules," true freedom, a year on my own—a blossoming. I live in an ancient, working-class neighborhood, which I adore; write about the current use of the guillotine; befriend an amazing couple who'd almost drowned in the Roaring Forties; travel with a gorgeous Midwestern homecoming queen; and hang out with some upper crust Parisians and some funny, enterprising expatriates. I take a screwed-up cruise on a crippled vessel in the English Channel, and spend a long, outlandish, violent evening with three of America's greatest writers. In sum, a rollicking, life-enhancing, year-long adventure.

Nowadays, there's no way I could push a lawnmower for a morning, swim in the surf for an hour, then play eighteen holes of golf, as I did in my teens. Nor could I, as in my twenties, sprint demonically up four flights of Greenwich Village stairs to get into bed with Natasha. Last year, when I took a walk in Paris, the streets seemed to be much farther apart than they were years ago ...

So I try to live with the changes, and to remember how my world sounded and smelled and tasted, and how it pleased and challenged those who were there.

One

LLOYD

As I've said, the most important luck is family luck.

If you have parents, grandparents, siblings, aunts, uncles, and cousins who care about you and look after you as you develop and learn, you're more fortunate than most.

And if your relations happen to be bright and talented and intriguing and keep you amused and add another dimension to your life thanks to *their* lives, you're even luckier.

* * *

My family was far from ordinary.

My complex father was an internationally known American art historian and museum director.

A glamorous aunt was coauthor of some of the sparklingest movies of Hollywood's Golden Age, and won a Pulitzer Prize for playwriting.

A great-aunt—genteel, Vassar-educated, stubborn, and Communist—was briefly one of the owners of the *Daily Worker*.

Another aunt was one of the first Yale women PhDs.

A college professor cousin wrote books about American history hailed by political conservatives.

Another cousin wrote speeches for Harry Truman.

A great-uncle wrote a Broadway comedy that was "as full of laughs as a shad is of bones."

A rich, lay-about cousin was convicted of arson.

A left-leaning writer cousin successfully defied Senator Joe McCarthy.

A millionaire socialist great-uncle wrote a muckraking, history-making exposé of the Standard Oil Company ...

And that, I'm glad to say, is *only half of the story.* All of those people were on my *father's* side of my family—and there were many interesting folks on my *mother's* side, too.

* * *

Like many Americans, I'm a mongrel, a mix of English, Welsh, Irish, and French. I'm a descendant of William Bradford, the *Mayflower* passenger and governor of the Plymouth Colony, and of three men who served in General Washington's Army. One of my mother's grandmothers was born in Ireland. In my background are the names Havens, Demarest, Wickes, Rossiter, Maverick, and Murphy. Those people included a preacher, a postmaster, a slave-owning farmer, doctors, lawyers, secretaries, sellers of real estate, captains of whaling ships, housewives, grocers, and individuals impossible to pigeonhole.

I loved my father, Lloyd Goodrich. He used to say that one of his aunts said that, as a newborn, he "looked foxy." As an adult, he did, sort of: shorter than average, always trim, he had brown, vaguely fox-colored hair, a short-cropped mustache, and a noteworthy nose; every artist who sketched or painted him (and quite a few did) emphasized it, and a writer once called it a "great prow." He was the youngest of five children, a workaholic, and a perfectionist: "I rewrite every page of my books ten times." In his twenties, he badly wanted to be a painter; when he failed, he had a nervous breakdown, went through psychoanalysis (rare in those days), then started writing about American art and wound up as the director of the world's greatest museum of American art, the Whitney, in New York; he was also the world's leading expert on the works of three great American artists. In his later years, people saw him as articulate, accomplished, and self-possessed; in fact, he was a lot more complicated than that.

* * *

Today, Nutley, New Jersey, is Tony Soprano territory and something of a joke, but in 1897, when Lloyd was born there, it was a pleasant, pretty village not far from New York: green lawns, tree-lined roads, comfortable houses, and a country club featuring archery and outdoor teas. Lloyd's father, Henry Wickes Goodrich (who died before I came along), was a modestly successful Wall Street lawyer. He was a kindly, genial man who probably should have been a teacher; his real loves were reading poetry to children in his big, turreted house and directing amateur play productions. During visits to museums, so that his five children could "appreciate color better," Henry had them face away from the pictures, then bend over and look upside down between their legs. Henry enjoyed brandy and cigars, and sitting on the piazza of the Players Club in New York, betting on the color of the next passing horse or pair of ladies' stockings.

My grandmother, Madeleine Lloyd Goodrich (who gave my father her maiden name as his first name; he, in turn, made it my middle name), was born in 1862, the daughter of a rigidly Calvinistic Dutch Reformed minister who made money in New Jersey real estate. I thought she was the perfect grandmother. She was small and slender, with humor and a strong will, as seen in a 1908 letter to her husband about a lazy hired man:

> I have been mowing the lawn. George abandoned his work at twelve, so I went out and in twenty minutes did more than he did in two hours ... Tell him you will not pay as long as he takes 2 ½ hours off ... He has today not even the excuse of the horse to feed, as the horse is away being shod.

The Nutley house Lloyd grew up in was dark-shingled and gray-trimmed, with a wraparound porch. As a kid, visiting on Christmas, I passed through a vestibule, stamping the snow off my galoshes, into a foyer that held heavy furniture, a few oil paintings, a stuffed moose head, and a grand piano. An unsunny "sun room" and a parlor were on either side. From there you moved into the big, comfortable living room—a glowing fireplace, hundreds of books, armchairs with antimacassars—then into the dining room, where the table could seat twenty. Upstairs were seven or eight bedrooms; above them were two servants' rooms.

Lloyd had three sisters and a brother.

The eldest was Constance, a thin, also beak-nosed intellectual who graduated from Vassar in 1911 with honors, taught English literature there, earned a PhD at Yale, and then contracted Parkinson's disease. For the rest of her life, she was a semi-invalid addicted to reading and ninety-minute walks. The last time I saw her, in her eighties, she asked me to buy three recent detective novels for her. They'd been published in German: "I haven't read enough German lately."

William—"Will"—was short and round-faced and always seemed resigned to failure. He was sent to Phillips Exeter Academy (perhaps to "make a man" of him?) and to Stevens Institute of Technology. His best moments were in World War I, when he was an enlisted man in the Navy, helping to stretch an antisubmarine net across Long Island Sound: I laughed at his stories about the screw-ups. He loved sailing, and owned a neat little cruising sloop. He never moved out of the Nutley house, living there with his widowed mother and his two wives (the first died) and managing the real estate his mother inherited. He developed a New Jersey accent ("moisten" came out "mersen"), and studied his ancestry devoutly. Rebelling against his family's liberalism, he became a radical conservative, worshipping Senator Joe McCarthy.

After Vassar, Caroline ("Tookey") happily married a Rhode Island businessman, Maxwell Huntoon; lived in a house as grand as the Nutley one; and had three children. She was good-looking and funny; I loved watching her facial contortions as she imitated the sounds of a 1920s vintage automobile hitting (but not killing) a dog. The car grinds steadily nearer; its horn toots a warning; the dog barks; tires squeal; the dog howls in pain ...

Of all of Lloyd's siblings, his favorite—and mine— was Frances, the playwright-screenwriter.

* * *

I thought that Frances—brown-haired, average-sized, with a handsome profile, always beautifully dressed, warm and generous—was amazing, the perfect image of glamour, romance, and the best of Hollywood's Golden Age. After graduating from Vassar in 1912, she played minor roles in stock companies and on Broadway. She later said she "wasn't very good," but bad actresses don't work as often as she did. She was divorced twice, from a handsome, alcoholic actor, then from the Dutch-born author Hendrik Willem van Loon, whose books popularizing human history sold an estimated six million copies. Then she met a ten-years-younger aspiring writer/actor named Albert Hackett.

Albert was lightly built, with a brown crewcut and an elfin, mischievous face. Starting at age five, he'd performed often on Broadway, mainly in comic roles. He offered to help on a play Frances was writing; it wasn't produced, but others were, and in 1931 they married. They turned out the scripts for some thirty Hollywood movies, including *The Thin Man*, *It's a Wonderful Life*, *Seven Brides for Seven Brothers*, *Easter Parade*, and *Father of the Bride*. The achievement they were proudest of was the stage version of *The Diary of Anne Frank*.

Frances and Albert were married for fifty-three years, until her death. They treated each other as equals, teased each other, and at times were models of sophistication. They regarded movie producers as stingy and tyrannical, and helped to found the Screen Writers Guild. Their dinner parties attracted many of Hollywood's brightest actors, directors, and writers. S. J. Perelman said they were "incredibly kind and generous people ... who take as dim a view as I do of this insane place." Ogden Nash wrote, "Everybody in Hollywood is nothing but codfish and halibut / Compared to Frances and Alibert." They once paid an $8,000 hotel bill for a drunken Dashiell Hammett and got him onto a plane for New York. They shared a Florida vacation house with Lillian Hellman, whose pot roast "tasted like a shag rug." When a young Jimmy Stewart's Hollywood bosses didn't renew his contract, they got him a role that probably saved his career. In the late thirties, their good friend Jim Cagney told them Hollywood wouldn't last: "When this picture stuff is over, we're going to have to go back to New York and work."

Frances and Albert hated writing sequels: the characters were boringly familiar. They did one for *Father of the Bride*; it was a hit, and MGM asked for yet another. They began reluctantly planning the script—

and then the husband of Joan Bennett (who played the bride's mother), suspecting that Bennett was having an affair with her agent, shot the agent.

"He shot him in the scrotum, in a parking lot," Frances recalled. "The publicity killed the second sequel."

"That saved us," Albert said. "He didn't kill him, but I imagine he ruined the affair."

Writing *The Diary of Anne Frank* was an ordeal, particularly for Frances: she had no children and was highly emotional, and Anne, the gifted, perceptive teenager who hid in an Amsterdam attic and died at Belsen, "became her daughter"; Frances wept whenever she spoke about her. The Hacketts wrote eight versions; grew close to Otto Frank, Anne's father; fought between themselves; and worked intensely with the director, Garson Kanin. After they visited the Amsterdam building where the Frank family hid, Frances wrote, "Very harrowing. Stood in Anne's room, stretched out my arms, touched walls on either side … a week of tears." The play ran on Broadway for seven hundred and seventeen performances, won the Pulitzer and every other prize, and has since been performed around the world countless times.

I spent some time—never enough—with Frances and Albert. In 1960, I drove through France and Switzerland with them. She called him "Hackett;" he referred to her as "The Madam" or "the lady I'm travelling with." After 1960, when they retired and moved to New York, they gave wonderful dinner parties. Lillian Hellman puffed cigarettes and looked grumpy; Harold Rome played "Sing Me a Song With Social Significance" on the piano. At their Martha's Vineyard summer house, I watched one of my nephews whack a ping pong ball into the back of James Cagney's neck (Cagney let out a gangsterish chuckle).

Lloyd's love of Frances was deep and lasting, but I always felt that, under the surface, Lloyd—eight years her junior—was competing with her. She was at the top of her field; he was going to get to the top of his (and he did). Having close, older family members who set high standards, the way Frances did, can be a stimulus; in Lloyd's case, it may have increased the almost compulsive need to *achieve* that he felt all his life.

* * *

Lloyd went to a grade school run by a family friend, then to Nutley High School. As a teenager, he read incessantly, drew bodies and faces, and wrote bad romantic poetry: "The moon is full and love is in the night / Love haunts the perfumed darkness everywhere." His father had gone to Amherst; Lloyd was accepted there. He would have been younger than the other freshmen; his father said, "Take a year off." Lloyd announced that his real ambition was to become a painter and enrolled in the Art Students League, in New York. In the end, he spent four years studying painting—and then realized he wasn't good enough to support himself. He never went to college, never earned a BA; but, thanks to his brains, curiosity, and non-stop reading, he was jam-packed with knowledge. In later years, wearing gorgeous caps and gowns, he was awarded honorary doctoral degrees by four different institutions.

Lloyd's earliest, best friend was Reginald Marsh, later famous for his paintings of raffish city life. Reg had a round, freckled face and red hair; his buddies called him Wig. He was shy and somewhat withdrawn. Everywhere he went, he carried a sketchbook; when I was a child, he sometimes drew me. Reg and Lloyd grew up as Nutley neighbors. In an odd twist, Reg, who was artistic talent personified, was sent to Yale to hit the books while Lloyd, who had no real artistic talent (but did have talent as a writer) studied painting. (At the League, Lloyd sometimes got sharp comments: "One of the finest teachers once took my drawing and rubbed it all out with a chamois cloth and began to draw it himself. I said, 'Mr. Bridgeman, I don't see it that way.' He said, 'Consult an oculist.'") Still living with his parents in Nutley, Lloyd was unhappy: "Here I am," a letter to Reg said, "farting around the house after Sunday dinner ... I swore that I'd hunt up a girl to fall in love with, but where is she? ... I'm wasting my youth ..." Lloyd and Reg sometimes served as non-singing extras at the Metropolitan Opera. In *Aida*, they and others marched across the stage in armor then raced around behind the scenery and marched again, creating the impression of an army. They hiked around New England, once covering seventy-two miles in a day and a half. Late in World War I, the Army rejected Lloyd because of a "heart murmur" (Lloyd had no heart problems later, and lived to be eighty-nine). To help the war effort, he and Reg worked for five months in a shipyard in Mystic, Connecticut, on the "bull gang," doing "everything anybody else didn't want to, like unloading freight cars."

One beautiful afternoon when I was around five, Lloyd and Reg took me sailing. I sat between them. A seagull flew over the boat, and drops of liquid hit my head. Self-conscious, fearing the worst, I snuck my hand up to check if the wetness was sticky. No, thank God. A minute later, another gull, and more liquid. I started to check my head again, but saw that Lloyd and Reg were trying not to laugh. Then Reg reached over the side, caught some drops of water in his fingers, and released them onto his own head. Even at that young age, I could feel, *Gee, these two guys really like one another.* Reg died far too young—in 1954, of a heart attack; for months, Lloyd was devastated.

In 1937, Reg was commissioned to paint fresco murals, showing a ship's arrival in New York Harbor, in the rotunda of the Customs House. With the Hacketts and Jimmy Cagney, Lloyd watched Reg at work, high up on a scaffold. Cagney climbed up for a closer look; to his annoyance, he was spotted, and was mobbed when he came down. Cagney complained often about overeager fans, but non-fans were galling, too. Some years later, the Hacketts introduced him to two reclusive Vermont farmers who didn't recognize him and asked where he came from. Cagney curtly replied, "California;" later, he was indignant: "Where I am *from*? Where am I *from*? Who're they trying to kid?"

At the Art Students League, Lloyd met Edmund Duffy, a New Jersey policeman's son whose political cartoons won three Pulitzer Prizes. Duffy was a fastidious dresser. He, Lloyd, and Reg took a trip in a car that broke down out in the country. They had to sleep in a ditch; before hanging his jacket on a tree limb, Duffy carefully draped it over a hanger he had in his suitcase. Drawing his cartoons, he worked quickly, Lloyd once visited him when he was drawing for the *Baltimore Sun*. They were going to the racetrack, but first Duffy had to do his daily cartoon. "He disappeared for half an hour," Lloyd said. "That drawing was one of his Pulitzer Prize ones."

A few years after their time at the League, Lloyd wrote a letter saying he'd been to his first professional baseball game with Duffy:

> Just before the game, ... somebody gave
> Babe Ruth a silver bat, life size. Then the
> Babe proceeded to strike out ... four times
> ... it certainly is a great game to watch ...
> those men seemed miraculous to me. Well
> do I remember how I always fumbled the
> ball, and struck out... Me for a nice quiet

game of golf, where you can think over
each shot, planning it carefully beforehand
and regretting it bitterly afterward.

Lloyd's father, Henry Goodrich, had two sisters.
One married a businessman, the other married an
Episcopal priest. Lloyd liked them all well enough, but
felt they weren't "progressive." However, one of the
businessman's sons interested him. This was Clinton
L. Rossiter 3rd, a professor in Cornell University's
Department of Government. He published a number of
well-regarded books on American History; one of them,
Seedtime of the Republic, is still used as a textbook.
Clinton's political views were conservative—which made
for lively arguments over pre-lunch martinis.

* * *

Madeleine Lloyd Goodrich (my grandmother) had
a sister and three brothers.

I recall John Calvin Lloyd as an affectionate, elderly
gentleman, seated outdoors on sunny mornings; white
linen golfing knickers, a panama hat. When I was four
or five, we played a game: I strolled with studied
nonchalance past his rocking chair, and he studiously
ignored me—but then caught my neck with his cane. He
was a coffee merchant, known as "the inventor of the
Yuban blend." His ancestor worship was sometimes
comical: "On my father's side," he wrote, "I am
descended from Goff, first lieutenant of Oliver
Cromwell, who, with the other two lieutenants, Dixwell
and Whalley, by direction of Oliver Cromwell,
superintended, in his name, the beheading of
Charles I."

I didn't know David Demarest Lloyd—he died at
age thirty-eight. He had many talents: he started as a
journalist in New York, moved to Washington and
became the private secretary of Supreme Court Chief

Justice Salmon B. Chase, then went on to write successful plays. One, mentioned earlier, was "as full of laughs as a shad of bones." The playbill said that the characters included "Tom Ripley, a young medical student who knows just how many bones you have in your body" and "Dr. Lane, proprietor of a private lunatic asylum, and strong on the medulla oblongata."

(David Demarest Lloyd's grandson, also named David Demarest Lloyd, was a lawyer who wrote two novels and went into government service, ultimately becoming President Harry S. Truman's friend, aide, and speechwriter. In early 1950, Senator Joseph McCarthy questioned David's loyalty—he belonged to several liberal organizations. This caused Truman to call a press conference and heatedly term McCarthy a pathological liar: "Does Senator McCarthy ever tell the truth? If so, I have not found it out.")

Caroline (Caro), the sister of Madeleine, John, and David, was a vivid personality—although always plainly dressed—with dark, almost fierce eyes. She graduated from Vassar in 1881, taught school, and then in Paris married an oddball "philosophical anarchist" and professional genealogist from Newburyport, Massachusetts, named Lothrop Withington. She divorced poor Lothrop—he turned out to have another wife in England—and he drowned in 1915 in the sinking of the *Lusitania*. She later married a Socialist schoolmaster, a quiet little man who once ran for Mayor of Newark, New Jersey; he died in 1925 while working on a collective farm in Russia. Caro joined the Communist Party in 1935 and wrote articles for the *Daily Worker*; in 1940, she became one of the paper's owners. This was a legal maneuver: under pressure from the House Un-American Activities Committee, the party tried to make itself look more patriotic by "selling" the paper for a brief time to three women of old American descent. Caro's radicalism caused heated arguments with her family. When reports of the horrors of Stalinist purges reached the U.S., Caro denounced them as "capitalist propaganda." She once wrote a letter to Eleanor Roosevelt, saying, in part, "Communists believe in the inevitable development of capitalism into socialism, a belief put into practice in the U.S.S.R. with glorious success."

When I was an infant, Aunt Caro made a great fuss over me (probably because she had no children of her own). Later, I often saw her walking across a seaside golf course in the early morning, her hair and skirt blowing in the wind, observing seagulls "pompously parading" (her words) while she gathered wild mushrooms for soup. Her relatives and many friends loved her, and watched with sympathy as she reacted to the 1939 Nazi-Soviet nonaggression pact; some said it "killed her—she died of a broken heart" (in fact, she did die a year later, at age eighty-one). From Caro, I learned Karl Marx's phrase, "From each according to his abilities, to each according to his needs"; it made sense to me then and it still does. I also believe that how a society treats its weakest citizens is a clear indicator of its health—so today's America is far from healthy.

If Caro's siblings didn't buy her convictions, most of them *did* buy those of the third brother, Henry Demarest Lloyd, an extraordinary man I never met (he died in 1903). He was a lawyer, journalist, editorialist, and author; his 1894 book, *Wealth Against Commonwealth*, exposing the machinations of the Standard Oil Company, has been called a muckraking classic; Henry himself has been called a "great champion of social and economic justice." He was born in New York in 1847, graduated from Columbia, briefly practiced law, and then moved to Chicago, where he wrote editorials for the *Chicago Tribune* and had the good sense to marry the wealthy daughter of one of the paper's owners. The marriage was happy and produced four sons. Henry dressed expensively, and had longish hair and a flowing mustache; his friends included Clarence Darrow, Jane Addams, Eugene Debs, and Booker T. Washington. In *Titan: The Life of John D. Rockefeller, Sr.*, Ron Chernow wrote that Henry

> was a literary troubadour for radical causes ... He once referred to himself as a "socialist-anarchist-communist-individualist-collectivist-cooperative-aristocratic democrat" ... He presented Rockefeller and his cohorts as brazen criminals ... His book had a profound and lasting impact ... Lloyd was a superb stylist with a political message: "Liberty produces wealth, and wealth destroys liberty" ... The noble experiment of democracy, he said, was being undermined by businessmen who had grown more powerful than the state and controlled its elected representatives.

I don't know about you, but to me that sounds a lot like what's going on today.

Thirty-nine years after *Wealth Against Commonwealth*, another American capitalist, Andrew Mellon, was muckraked in another exposé, *Mellon's Millions*, which has been described this way:

> The author was an acknowledge anti-capitalist ... he described the blatant favoritism that the State Department had shown Gulf Oil ... He also detailed the entrenched anti-labor attitudes, which he insisted existed in all Mellon companies. Finally, he insisted that through his

extensive investments and his multifarious family trusts and connections, Andrew Mellon had become a manipulative malefactor, unaccountable to anyone.

That makes *Mellon's Millions* sound a lot like *Wealth Against Commonwealth*—right?

The fact is, the author of *Mellon's Millions* was Henry Lloyd's grandson-in-law, Harvey O'Connor.

I knew Harvey O'Connor and his wife, Jessie Lloyd, well. They were wonderful—intelligent, energetic, humorous. She was thin and shorthaired, with big eyes behind thick glasses, and was eccentric: once, while vacationing in Texas, she asked a Rhode Island neighbor to get her tea strainer from her house and mail it to her. Harvey was a pipe-smoker with bright brown eyes, reddish hair, and a mustache. Jessie had money thanks to Henry Lloyd's marriage, so they could travel, support liberal causes, and live in beautiful places—but never extravagantly. Their servants ate dinner with them. Harvey wrote other controversial books, including *The Guggenheims* and *The Empire of Oil*. He and Jessie adopted two children. Jessie loved square dancing and folk singing; an evening at their house might include both do-see-do and a performance by their close, magical friend, Pete Seeger; I can still see him smiting his banjo to lead the singing of *Where Have All the Flowers Gone?*

In 1953, two of Senator Joseph McCarthy's cohorts found copies of some of Harvey's books in overseas U.S. Information Services libraries, and he was ordered to appear before the senator's notorious committee. When McCarthy asked if he was a member of the Communist Party (he wasn't), he refused to answer, citing the First Amendment, which guarantees freedom of speech. McCarthy accused him of contempt of

Congress (Harvey, eyes twinkling, called it "contempt of McCarthy"), and he was tried and sentenced to a year in jail (the conviction was reversed by a higher court). McCarthy called Harvey his "most contumacious" witness. "I considered that quite a compliment," Harvey said. "I didn't know what it meant, so I looked it up." (It means "insubordinate, stubbornly disobedient.") Few people forced to appear before McCarthy asked for their witness fee. Harvey had to write several times, but finally a check came, signed personally by McCarthy; Harvey endorsed it over to a civil rights group. About the whole experience, he said, "The Bill of Rights is just a piece of paper unless people fight for it."

Many Lloyds, obviously, were mavericks. Some were also partly Mavericks—in 1903, William Lloyd, one of Henry Demarest Lloyd's sons, married Lola Maverick, the granddaughter of Samuel Maverick, a Texas founding father whose unbranded calves, roving off his ranch, gave rise to the word "maverick" ("an independent individual who refuses to conform with his group"). Some Mavericks have been famous partly for being mavericks—for example, Maury Maverick Jr., a civil liberties lawyer, Texas legislator, newspaper columnist, and born iconoclast, once escorted presidential candidate John F. Kennedy through the Alamo, where revered Texans made their last stand against Mexican troops. Behind schedule, Kennedy asked Maury Jr. to lead him out the back door. "There is no back door," Maury replied. "That's why they're all heroes."

Jessie Lloyd O'Connor was half-Maverick. A sister of hers, Mary Maverick Lloyd, was a gentle, humorous soul who lived in Paris for many years (and helped me greatly there; more about that later). From her house in Paris, Mary ran the International Registry of World Citizens and helped to support the cause of world government. Another brainy, vivacious Maverick descendant, Florence Kelley, a 1937 Yale Law School graduate, became administrative judge of New York State's Family Court. For thirteen years, Florrie was the head of the criminal branch of the Legal Aid Society. She once asked a new client, "You're the man who robbed the delicatessen?" and he replied, "No, Ma'am, I'm the one who pushed the woman out the thirteenth story window."

Inevitably, in this family of idealistic strivers and achievers, there was a lamb of a darker hue. As far as I know, Carrington ("Cang") Lloyd never—except for service in the Navy in World War II—worked a day in his life. Good-natured, tall, and good-looking, he spent most of his life in Rhode Island and Florida. He owned boats, and courted one of his three wives offshore ("With the engine off, we'd go below. No one could sneak up on us, because we'd hear them coming"). With another wife, Cang took a very expensive cruise to Europe on the *Queen Elizabeth II.* Back in the U. S. he phoned home: was the remodeling of the kitchen finished? Told that it wasn't, the Lloyds quickly arranged to stay on board for another cruise to Europe ("The Verandah Bar on that ship is fabulous"). On Halloween when he was 39, after many drinks, Cang and a 17-year-old fellow-prankster set fire to a ten-room, deserted house that stood on an island in a river in Westport, Massachusetts. It was an attractive target for Halloween because it had once belonged to a religious group called the Holy Ghost Mission; the teenager and the middle-ager rowed out to it with a can of gasoline. In Superior Court, they received suspended, year-and-a-half sentences for arson, and Cang paid the owner of the completely destroyed building $7,500.

* * *

Readers will have noticed that both the Goodrich and Lloyd families contained many writers. Growing up among them had an effect on me; writing seemed exciting, glamorous, and worthy. Until I actually started doing it, I didn't realize how hard it was—but by then, I was hooked.

* * *

After four years at the Art Students League, Lloyd faced an unpleasant truth: he couldn't make it as a painter. Almost all of the paintings and drawings he did then have disappeared. I own a few oil landscapes; they're pleasant, but they lack excitement and originality. His drawings—of faces and nudes—were stiff and uninspired. More than most people, he knew good art from bad, and the realization that he shouldn't keep on trying hit hard. In his words, he suffered

> a nervous crisis, a depression, a melancholia ... It was so severe that I needed psychiatric help ... My analyst had been analyzed by Freud. I was analyzed for about two years, and this was the most educational experience of my entire life ... I think I came out of it a much better adjusted person ... Analysis makes it absolutely essential that you should become aware of your unconscious problems. It's tremendously powerful, with the most vital motivation, which is preservation of one's mental health. I ascribe to analysis the fact that I went on to become a writer. The clarification of mind that came with analysis helped me a great deal to express myself ...

During Lloyd's analysis, he met my mother, Edith Havens (I loved her, too). In the summer of 1922, he wrote her a letter, saying, in part,

> Sometimes when I think of that L. G. with the scraggly mustache who made love to you last winter, I think he was a pretty poor creature. He had a terrible opinion of himself; he cared much more for the emotions Edith Havens aroused in him than he did for Edith Havens herself; he was inclined to be theatrical, to sentimentalize ... I don't know whether the new L. G. is any better, but at least I think he is more real, more honest with himself and with the said Edith Havens. Also, he has shaved off his mustache, which alone is worth the price of admission, as they say in dime museums.

Lloyd grew a new mustache and wore it for the rest of his life. Not only was he changing during his analysis, he was also fiercely in love with "the said Edith Havens," and wrote her letter after letter. One, a fourteen-pager, contained sketches of himself in sad and happy moods (before and after spending an evening with her); a hand-drawn calendar with the days when he hadn't seen her tinted gray and those when he had tinted pink; and, pressed between the pages, two small, pink flowers. He added,

> Edith Havens is lovely, and yet look how she treats that poor Lloyd Goodrich! He's crazy about her, and she knows it, yet she behaves as if he were the dirt under her feet; if he had any spunk, he'd leave her cold.

"Edith and I were engaged without really knowing it," Lloyd said years later, "until—well, we knew it ... I married her about two years from the time we first met. My analysis terminated, and I married her within about a month."

Two

EDITH

My mother was two years younger than Lloyd, brown-haired, blue-eyed, a trifle overweight, and beautiful, with a delicate, retroussé nose that neatly complimented Lloyd's beak. When they met, she was making $45 a week teaching costume design at a YWCA in Brooklyn, and he was making $35 as a book company editorial assistant. They were married in January 1924.

Edith's parents, Edwin Taylor Havens and Lilly Murphy, died before I was born, and she didn't talk about them a lot—maybe because, once married, she was swept into the Goodrich-Lloyd establishment, whose history and ego-power overshadowed her own family's. Edith said that her father was "a printer;" perhaps he owned a printing company. She also said he was an avid bicyclist, often taking part in one hundred-mile-per-day events. He descended from a numerous tribe of Havenses who helped to settle small, green Shelter Island, at the eastern end of Long Island. Lilly's parents emigrated from Ireland; Edith said they missed the first ship they'd booked passage on because their send-off party was too good. According to Edith, when her father died, he left very little money, but I wonder about that: in the mid-twenties, the widowed Lilly took at least two pleasure trips to Europe. Sadly, she could be a bore. During a trip to Italy, she sent Edith a six-page letter, from fascinating Florence, with almost two pages devoted to a game of bridge ("By some streak of luck, I held good cards and we won three rubbers running which included big slams and little slams").

Edith grew up in Brooklyn and Mountain Lakes, New Jersey; she went to a private, all-girls high school in Boonton, New Jersey. The classes were small; the headmaster was an Episcopal priest; Edith played basketball and was editor-in-chief of the school magazine. In that publication, a classmate wrote that Edith had "a will of her own and knows how to use it." The classmate added, "She has lately tried to cross off a few years of her life by cutting her hair, and never was there such excitement as on the morning when this was learned by the amazed students." Hoping to work in fashion, Edith went briefly to Parsons School of Design. Then she got her "Y" job; then she met Lloyd.

Edith had two brothers. Valentine was athletic and arrestingly handsome, with a cleft chin. At Rutgers, he broke records as a hurdler; he did the same as a Rhodes Scholar at Oxford. He married a classically beautiful Englishwoman, then went to law school. He did well as a tax specialist, and spent summers in East Hampton, Long Island, where he belonged to the Maidstone Club and bought real estate that he sold to friends at bargain prices. "My God," Val's son (Val also had a daughter) sometimes says, "If he'd hung onto that property, we'd be billionaires today!" Val's only failures were in marriage: he was divorced three times. His shorter, plainer-looking brother Donald never jumped over hurdles, but he also became a top-level lawyer; his marriage, to a pianist who taught advanced courses at Juilliard, lasted 'til his death, and produced three children. Don's specialty was admiralty law. Ironically, he died at sea of a heart attack, while crossing the Atlantic for a well-deserved vacation: he'd just spent many stressful weeks cleaning up the legal mess following the *Andrea Doria–Stockholm* collision. Val and Don, the two lawyers, loved arguing—and not just about professional matters. Lloyd sometimes joined in, and I still recall the three debating politics after a Christmas dinner when I was a teenager. I told myself, *I'm in the presence of genius* (but my epiphany may have been champagne-induced).

Edith loved her brothers, and she also loved her uncle Bert and her cousins—the siblings Beckwith, Henrietta, and Gertrude.

Albert ("Bert") Gallatin Havens was a lifelong bachelor. In his twenties, he started a lumber company. An uncle of his embezzled several thousand dollars and fled to Maine: no more lumber company. Bert became a successful banker. He dressed well; owned expensive cars; and during European visits, did landscapes in watercolor. He too died of a heart attack—at age sixty-eight, in France. He doted on Edith, sending her countless letters and describing her in verse; I suspect he was a bit in love with her. In one poem, dedicated to "The Rose of Roses, From Her Beau Ideal," he said she was "A goddess, not of Rome or Greek, / Her nerve and knowing all bespeak / The blood of Celtic giant."

In 1911, Edith's cousin, Beckwith Havens, born in 1890, was taught to fly by the pioneer pilot Glenn Curtis in aircraft that looked like Leonardo da Vinci sketches. Like Valentine, Beckwith was handsome. He flew at county fairs in thirteen states and in Cuba (the mayor of Havana gave him a watch decorated with pearls). Concerning his flying at Ashland, Wisconsin, a local lady reported, "The fair maidens of our town were all agog, for now they had a new hero to idolize—Beckwith Havens, and Douglas Fairbanks' name was relegated to second place." Beckwith was the first to fly across Long Island Sound, and the first to fly an amphibious plane across the U.S. During World War I, he was a test pilot, during World War II, a Commander in the Navy, running an air base in Cuba (still wearing his pearl-studded Havana watch?). Meantime, he was an executive in various aircraft companies. In his sixties, Beckwith sometimes visited Edith at teatime, and I would listen to his jaw-dropping stories. One concerned a youthful exhibition flight in Enid, Oklahoma, in a plane as fragile as a child's kite. The afternoon was dangerously windy, so Beckwith—as he later told a magazine,

> kept stalling. I was walking over the field, partly to kill time and partly to look for gopher holes, when a buckboard caught up with me, with the horses driven ... by the local sheriff, complete with six-gun and belt. He looked down and asked, 'Son, are you gonna fly?' 'Sure,' I said ... he drove me back to the grandstand ... and raised his hand to quiet the roaring crowd, and shouted, 'Give this boy a chance. It's his last ride before he gets to ride with the undertaker!' I made the flight and got an enthusiastic ovation.

Beckwith had two accomplished sisters; I knew them slightly. Gertrude, for a time an architect with a fashionable 1920's firm, married Dr. Barton Cookingham, a surgeon who joined the French Red Cross in World War I, became a colonel in the Serbian Army, and for his medical services was awarded the Serbian Order of the Golden Eagle, an honor rarely bestowed on foreigners. In spite of heavy drinking, he helped to found a hospital near Rhinebeck, New York. Henrietta, known as Mouse thanks to the shape of her ears, attended Barnard College, sold fashion illustrations, then married Harold Roig, whose success at the importing-shipping company W. R. Grace pleased her mightily (her *full* childhood nickname was Money-Mad Mouse the Multi-Millionaire).

Edith was proud of her Havens ancestors. One reached America from Wales in 1635 and settled on Shelter Island; for many generations, Havenses were among the gentry there. In 1743, Nicoll Havens built a large house called "Heartsease." There were two orchards, outhouses, barns, a blacksmith shop, and a windmill. Ironically—considering the house's name—Nicoll owned fourteen slaves (Edith was *not* proud of that). Many Havenses served in island government, as town supervisor, town clerk, constable-and-collector, and fence viewer; one served for four years in the U.S. Congress. During the Revolutionary War, the British ransacked the homes of two Havenses, taking fowling pieces, a sword with a silver hilt, some tea, a watch, and a coat. Four Havenses commanded whaling ships; one went to California during the Gold Rush; another, described in a history of Shelter Island as a "most lovable character," kept a general store where "the farmers met the soldiers and sailors, home from camp and sea, and listened to strange tales of happenings on whaling and clipper ships, and on Civil War battlefields."

* * *

Edith knew she was beautiful, but sometimes coyly denied it. Before they were married, she wrote to Lloyd that she'd visited Arthur William Brown, whose illustrations for stories by Ring Lardner and F. Scott Fitzgerald appeared in leading magazines. His studio, she wrote, was "more of a workroom, for there was nothing attractive about, except himself and his work. But here's the comedy: he wants me to pose for him. Can you stand it? Me, with this cross that I bear in the way of a nose? Won't it be funny to break out in the *Saturday Evening Post*?"

As newlyweds, Lloyd and Edith lived in a small apartment on Middagh Street in Brooklyn Heights. There was a whorehouse nearby, and they once watched a police raid: the cops poured into the front door while the girls and the johns, half naked and obviously tipped off, popped up onto the building's roof and scurried down into the building next door.

Lloyd was now working unhappily in the religious books department of a major publishing house, Macmillan. As happens at publishing houses, crackpots showed up. In July 1924, he wrote to Edith:

> An old reverend came in today and said
> he was going to write a shorter Bible, in
> which he wanted a novel arrangement of
> the type—like this:
>> In six days the Lord created
>> The on and earth and heaven
>> Seventh day He rested.
> See the idea? The first line you read left
> to right, the second right to left, the third
> left to right, etc. He said it was much more
> restful: you don't have to snap your eyes
> back to the beginning of the next line.

After leaving Macmillan, Lloyd started writing about art for the *New York Times* and various periodicals; he seems to have decided that since he couldn't become a painter, this was a way of remaining in a world he loved—and of course, his Art Students League training helped him to understand the artistic process. Edith encouraged his writing. In many ways, she was his collaborator: in the evening, while she mended his socks (she loved sewing), he read that day's writing to her, waiting for comments. They were married for sixty years, until she died of a heart attack. They were well matched, and although they occasionally fought—what married couple doesn't?—they were happy. He was a bit of a hypochondriac, and had fits of depression; I particularly recall two terrible weeks when the editor of one of his books wasn't returning his calls.

Edith had a temper that could flare up fiercely. That frightened me when I was little; she jokingly put the blame on being half-Irish. When she called people "conventional"—meaning unimaginative, stodgy, not interested in the arts—they were damned forever. She and Lloyd both smoked (never more than three cigarettes a day; they liked the smell), and enjoyed evening martinis. Edith was careful not to overindulge, recalling a wedding reception where, after too much champagne, she threw her white gloves into the toilet and flushed them down. She was an optimist—when I failed at a task, she'd say, "You've learned something." She was also an excellent cook; no leg of lamb was ever better than hers, with herbs and deeply embedded garlic slivers. Lloyd had no interest in machines, and was the only person I ever knew who never learned to drive a car, so Edith did the chauffeuring. She liked driving, but did it badly—the car jerked and paused, and was often in the middle of the road. Even when Lloyd was working at the Whitney Museum, money was a problem—curators, even directors, then earned almost nothing—so I had to have scholarships through school and college. Lloyd and Edith's letters often mentioned books. With F. Scott Fitzgerald in mind, Lloyd addressed one of his "To the Beautiful from the Damned (Fool)." In one of hers, she asked,

> Isn't *Swann's Way* extraordinary? I think you are courageous to tackle it in French … How I enjoy it. Just as I did *War and Peace*—every line is precious. You want to go Oh so slowly and make it last. I find myself feeling the size of the book

ahead of me to read, and rejoicing in its very bulk.

* * *

Lloyd and Edith were zealous museum-goers, and knew a lot about American art (naturally) and about the Old Masters. Part of that European knowledge came in 1927-'28, when they spent a year abroad, going over on the *De Grasse*. A French Line publicity release announced that among the ship's passengers were eighteen chorus girls

> from the *Ziegfeld Follies* and *Rio Rita*, who will appear in a new Revue ... at the Moulin Rouge in Paris. Among them are two ... against whose leaving *Rio Rita* Ziegfeld began restraining action in the courts ... Another interesting passenger is Lloyd Goodrich, Associate Editor of *The Arts* magazine, who is sailing with Mrs. Goodrich for a year's study.

Lloyd and Edith must have loved the chorus girls; I can see them all laughing together. The Goodrichs spent part of their European time with Reg Marsh and his wife, Betts Burroughs, who had gone over a year earlier. Betts was a sculptor; her father, a curator at the Metropolitan Museum, gave the Marshes letters introducing them to French museum officials. Concerning one meeting, Reg wrote,

> Monsieur Guiffrey ... at the Louvre ... asked us to name any master whose drawings we should care to see. At the word "Rembrandt," officials produced chairs, special tables, reading glasses, whereby we could examine, breathe upon,

touch, hold up to our gaze the actual drawings, unframed, from the magic hand of the master. Following this, the servants discreetly retired, and although the impulse was great, we made away with none of them.

Reg added that Monsieur Guiffrey "kindly wrote us a letter to the distinguished conservator of the Chateau of Chantilly":

The most beautiful chateau ... with towers and spires, long walls, high walls, thick walls, ramparts, a moat, a lake, gardens ... It's magical ... The concierge greets us with "Get the hell out." After a two-franc piece, a little, white-haired Frenchman in a long black coat guides us through banquet halls, other halls, all very elaborate ... and then into the library. There with much opening of doors, cases, and cabinets, he draws forth a box, unlocks, removes satin pillows and reveals the most wonderful book, the *Très Riches Heures du Duc de Berry*. This book, made in 1416, is illustrated with the loveliest colored drawings you have ever seen! Grand, grand things, and then he remarked, "You are among the very, very few who have been admitted the perusal of this book."

The Marshes thought Paris was "the loveliest place on earth;" so did the Goodrichs. Edith visited bookstores, trying, in her stumbling French, to get them to carry *The Arts*. They lived in a little Left Bank hotel; the rates were modest, but so were the amenities: an unglazed window in the bathroom, which was shared with others—let in wintry air. (The hotel, on the rue de Verneuil, became almost a Goodrich tradition: I stayed there in 1951—the bathroom window had been glazed— and in 2008.) One day Lloyd and Edith walked twelve miles, exploring Paris; later, they took two long bicycle trips. The rest of the time, they looked at pictures.

"The Louvre was a great discovery," Lloyd said later, "like reading the history of art through the eyes. Going to Italy was the greatest kick I had with the art of the past ... We just looked and looked and looked ... I hated to come back. Just the physical look of New York was like having left an ordered and happy milieu to find yourself in a kind of jungle." He added that the art business then thriving in Paris was also a jungle: "It was extremely corrupt. The critics were all bought. You'd read a glowing account of some young artist, and you'd know it had been paid for. This ... didn't occur in the United States. The least hint of payment for criticism would absolutely put you out of running."

* * *

Back in New York, one of the art magazines Lloyd wrote for sent him to Greenwich Village, to the left-leaning New School for Social Research, to interview Jose Clemente Orozco, the politically radical Mexican painter. Orozco was painting murals in the school cafeteria, depicting a gathering of all the world's races, with Gandhi and Lenin seated at a "peace table." When Lloyd arrived, the fresco plaster was drying fast, and the model for the Caucasian race hadn't shown up, so Orozco quickly painted Lloyd into the composition. "There I am at the peace table," Lloyd once said, "a very good likeness. I'm very proud of it." During the McCarthy era, curtains covered the murals. Today, the room is no longer the cafeteria, but a special-events meeting place called The Orozco Room, with the murals proudly and fully displayed.

* * *

Lloyd and Edith moved from Brooklyn Heights into Manhattan around the time I was born (1930; my sister, Madeleine, came along three years later). I've been told that I was a solemn baby; exhibiting me after my bath to dinner guests, my nursemaid, Pearl, used to announce, "Ladies and gentlemen, Judge Goodrich." As parents, Lloyd and Edith were "modern," teaching Maddy and me to use adult language; I learned to say "bowel movement" at an early age.

Childhood holidays had flavor. Thanksgiving meant an exciting trip by subway, Hudson River Ferry, and the Erie Railroad out to Nutley, to visit the stuffed moose head in the big Goodrich house. As per tradition, our various relatives and we would chant, as the cook brought the turkey (also stuffed) into the dining room, "He has gobbled his last gobble, and now we will gobble him." Waiting for the train that would take us back to the ferry, I would put a penny on a track for flattening. At Christmas, in the New York apartment, the tree was decorated with honest-to-God candles. Lloyd went to exercise classes at the nearby Young Men's Hebrew Association. Someone there had a sense of humor: to warm up, the exercisers marched to the beat of a piano playing *Onward Christian Soldiers*. Lloyd amused us with quotes he'd picked up God-knows-where: "If we had ham, we could have ham and eggs, if we had eggs" and "How do your symptoms sargastuate?" Although they didn't care about sports, Lloyd took me to hockey and baseball games and played catch with me, and Edith took Maddy and me to an ice skating rink called— yes—Gay Blades. We went to Abbott and Costello flicks, Larry Adler and Paul Draper harmonica-and-dance matinees (both performers were avid liberals), and to

Hellzapoppin', a blend of low-comedy gags and ear-splitting sound effects; at age ten, it was perfect. Around that time, I asked Edith if she loved me as much as she loved Lloyd; she answered, "Yes, but in a different way." I didn't realize it then, but that was my introduction to sex. In my New York preteen years, I was taken hundreds of times to museums to look at paintings. Once my free time became my own, I seldom visited the temples of art; I'd been "museumed out." The feeling has persisted. In a foreign city, I don't head for the Hermitage or the Louvre; I roam the streets, to watch people and try to figure them out.

* * *

In 1930, Gertrude Vanderbilt Whitney—rich, generous, and an accomplished sculptor—started the Whitney Museum of American Art. The director, Mrs. Juliana Force, hired Lloyd, as part of the four-person staff, to write exhibition catalogues, press releases, and books about historical American artists. His job title was "Research Curator" ("which is ridiculous," he once said, "because you can't curate research"). Today, the Whitney resides in a bold, handsome building on Madison Avenue at 75th Street, designed by Marcel Breuer and sometimes called "an upside-down ziggurat." When Lloyd was hired, the museum occupied a neighborly, unobtrusive structure in Greenwich Village. The contrast between the two buildings says a lot about how the museum has changed over the years. While remaining true to its mission—to showcase whatever is deemed best in contemporary American art—the museum (like American art itself) has evolved in style from homey to assertive, from being like a quiet country fair to having big-city, audience-grabbing flash. "Flash" rhymes with "cash"—upon which, these days, election to the museum's governing body increasingly depends. In certain circles, Whitney trusteeship means making it socially; interestingly, two recent trustees have spent time in prison. (One of them, Dennis Kozlowski, of Tyco fame, was asked on CBS's *Sixty Minutes*, "Were you asked to join the Whitney board because of your money?" He laughed, and replied, "I assume it wasn't because of my knowledge of art.") Throughout the Whitney Museum's history, Lloyd was essential. It may seem surprising that someone so art-oriented could prove to be an effective administrator, but Lloyd was a complex man of many talents and interests.

* * *

In 1943, because the trustees were uncertain about the future, the Whitney Museum announced that it was going to move uptown and merge with the Metropolitan Museum. The Whitney's collection would be melded into the Met's, and a spacious Whitney Wing would be built. Five years later, serious discussions began. Lloyd told an oral historian that the Met's director, Francis Henry Taylor, was an "old friend"—"brilliant, combative, articulate, and somewhat fanatical about the contemporary art scene." Roland Redmond, the Met's president, invited Taylor, Lloyd, and Herman More, then the Whitney's director, to dinner at the Brook Club, a shiny-mahogany, candelabraed WASP haven, to work out the details of the deal. Lloyd said that "Everything was very cordial and pleasant, through dessert. About ten o'clock ... began an attack by Francis, participated in by our host, on modern art in general, and specifically on the Whitney's policies ...The implication was we didn't know what went on in America ... we concentrated on Greenwich Village and advanced art; strange people in dungarees visited our shows ... It got to be hammer-and-tongs ... we began to think, 'What are we doing? We're agreeing to join an institution that's hostile to modern art' ... our trustees broke off the agreement. I think it would have happened anyway, but the Brook Club incident was the precipitating thing."

Lloyd became the Whitney's director in 1958. Like Harvey O'Connor, he had trouble with witch hunters. In 1959, the United States Information Agency (USIA) sent the first-ever exhibition of 1928-1959 American art to Moscow; Lloyd was on the selection committee. There was a furor in Washington, led by a congressman who said that of the sixty-seven artists chosen, thirty-four had "records of affiliation with Communist fronts." At a press conference, President Eisenhower said he didn't know how the selection committee had been appointed. Lloyd wrote the president, pointing out that Eisenhower himself had approved the appointments, and sent the letter to several newspapers. McCarthyism was now on the wane, and the press reaction was, "This is ridiculous. We're not sending the artists, we're sending their art."

"The attendance at the show in Moscow," Lloyd said, "was enormous. The public reaction was incomprehension and some hostility, but also simple curiosity... The USIA had produced a fully illustrated catalogue in Russian, with an introduction by me. The high priest of Socialist realism, Vladimir Kemenov, wrote the most complete critique, reading much like the diatribes against modern art by our own archconservatives. Throughout, he paid his respects to me as an apologist for corrupt capitalist art."

As director, Lloyd dealt with some unusual people. For several years, Jacqueline Kennedy was a trustee. She couldn't remember the names of fellow trustees, so at meetings she sat beside Lloyd, whispering into his ear, "Who's that?" From the White House, Lady Bird Johnson asked Lloyd to get the Texas artist Peter Hurd to send slides of his work—the president was thinking of hiring Hurd to paint his official portrait. Lady Bird told Lloyd not to mention LBJ's name—"If we wind up not giving Hurd this important job, he'll be terribly disappointed"—so he had to say to Hurd, who was planning a vacation, "Forget that. When you learn who the sitter is, you'll be glad." After receiving the slides, Lady Bird wrote Lloyd a misspelled note saying, "The president and I are pouring over the slides" ("Probably bourbon and branch water," Lloyd said). Hurd got the job, and painted LBJ's ears life-size; LBJ hated the portrait, asking visitors, "Did you ever see anything so ugly?"

* * *

Through the years, Edith and Lloyd got to know more and more people connected to the Whitney. As a little kid, I went to exhibition openings and watched fascinated as tweed-jacketed, gregarious painters and sculptors gulped down drinks and hors d'oeuvres (for the less successful, they were dinner), swapped jokes and shop talk, and roared with laughter. Even better were the after-opening parties in Mrs. Force's elegant apartment, on the top floor or the Eighth Street building. She had eclectic taste, and her rooms were decorated with antiques, crystal chandeliers, knickknacks, and animal-skin rugs. Lloyd once said that Mrs. Force was "highly sociable. She loved people. She had very strong likes and dislikes, and she was one of the most amusing talkers I ever heard.... The social temperature rose ten degrees when she came into a room. She was sometimes cruel in her humor, but she was never dull." I recall her as short, full-figured, perfumed, expensively dressed, elaborately coifed and made up, and jangly and sparkly— rings, earrings, pins, brooches, necklaces. I liked her a lot, especially because, if I got sick, she'd send me a book to read in bed.

Among Lloyd and Edith's favorite people were two of the museum's trustees, Flora Miller and Flora Miller Biddle, daughter and granddaughter of the founder. The

Goodrichs saw the art dealers Edith Halpert and Betty Parsons often; collector friends included Maxim Karolik, a Russian-born singer who married a rich Proper Bostonian roughly twenty years older and put together a famous collection of American primitive art. (Concerning the overweight, 1930-'40s society hostess Elsa Maxwell, Karolik used to say, in his heavy Russian accent, "Her vaist is busted, and her bust is vaisted.") They enjoyed the architectural historian Henry Russell Hitchcock and James Johnson Sweeney, the first director of the Guggenheim Museum, who told Lloyd that the Guggenheim's architect, Frank Lloyd Wright, hadn't planned a big enough elevator. "When I told Wright we needed more space for our large artworks," Sweeney said, "he told me, 'Sell them.'" They had many painter and sculptor friends: Raphael and Moses Soyer, Peggy Bacon, Isabel Bishop, Yasuo Kuniyoshi, and Al Hirschfeld and his wife Dollie, who gave great parties in their East Ninety-Fifth Street house, where the walls wore Hirschfeld's live-wire drawings of theatrical celebrities. The collector William Burden's spacious apartment featured a six-inch-deep, water-filled "reflecting pool." At their New Years' Day parties, I stood near it, patiently waiting for guests to accidentally step into it. A number of artists, including Andrew Wyeth, Hans Hoffman, Elie Nadelman, and Willem de Kooning, gave works to Lloyd and Edith.

At the Whitney, Lloyd got to know the paintings of Edward Hopper, and felt that "a new vision and a new viewpoint on the contemporary world had appeared in American art. Through the years, each successive work has confirmed that conviction." Hopper and his wife Jo were grateful for the enthusiasm; after Hopper's death, Jo gave a treasure trove of drawings, paintings, and sketchbooks to the museum. I met Hopper several times. He seemed to me as enigmatic as his paintings; his silences were monumental. Until his later years, his income was small, and he and Jo lived frugally. In winters, he carried the coal for the potbellied stove in their Washington Square apartment up four flights of stairs. They spent summers in a house on Cape Cod. One summer, they adopted a stray cat and fed it their table scraps. Returning from a trip, they found the cat gone and a dead seagull outside the kitchen door; Jo laughed and said she guessed it was the animal's parting contribution to their larder. Jo was eccentric; although her figure was far from inspiring, she insisted that Hopper use her as his model. In 1961, Frances and Albert Hackett bought a large Hopper oil painting showing a young, slender nude with large, up-springing breasts, looking mournfully out a bedroom window. Typically, Hopper had given the picture a no-frills title: *A Woman in the Sun.* The Hacketts called it—privately— *Jo Glorified,* and Jo wrote them saying that *she* called it *The Sorrowful Sinner,* and regretted that Hopper hadn't painted a pair of men's shoes under the bed.

* * *

Lloyd retired as director in 1968. In 1979, the American Academy of Arts and Letters gave him its Distinguished Service to the Arts Award. As part of the lengthy awards program, John Updike delivered a talk titled *Hawthorne's Religious Language.* Of all the boring speeches I've ever heard, that was the most boring. The academy's two hundred and fifty members are distinguished writers, painters, sculptors, composers, and architects. Maybe a hundred of them sat on the stage, behind Updike, facing the audience. As they fell asleep, one by one, you could hear whispers: "There goes So-and-So, who won the Nobel Prize ... There goes Such-and-Such, who won two Pulitzers ..."

* * *

When Lloyd died, in 1987, the *New York Times* said:

> A key figure in the art world for decades, Mr. Goodrich pursued his passion for advancing America's indigenous art, not only as director... but as the author of many books ... and as a frequent public spokesman on issues concerning the importance of the visual arts in America. He wrote biographies and monographs on many of America's greatest artists, about whom he was a leading authority ... he guided the museum's ... transition from an essentially private institution into a public one ... He also presided over the construction of the museum's present quarters.... He sat on the editorial boards of art magazines and on advisory panels for the New York State Council on the Arts and the Fine Arts Advisory Committee to the White House.... In his public pronouncements and advocacy of American art throughout his career, Mr. Goodrich left much of his mark.

* * *

For several days in the summer of 1937, Lloyd tramped up and down Beacon Hill, in Boston, carrying a notebook and a big, boxy camera, shuttling between the homes of five sisters named Hooper, all of whom owned watercolors by Winslow Homer. Lloyd was doing research for a catalogue raisonné of the Boston-born artist's works, and the sisters opened their doors to let him document their collections. He also saw collections in New York, and wrote to Edith about one visit,

Mr. Pomroy owns Homer's "Camp Fire"
... a nice old fellow ... no chest at all.
Took off his coat, showing beautiful pair
of suspenders. Member of Stock Exchange
... Showed me "Camp Fire." Wonderful
thing ... A camp fire in the foreground—
behind, a shelter with two men ... I never
saw a picture that gave you the feeling of
night in the woods like that ... It's never
been reproduced or even photographed ...
Pomroy gave me a cigar. If all the collectors
do that, I'll die of cancer of the tongue,
like General Grant.

In 1944, Lloyd published a long monograph on
Homer; he continued gathering information until his
death. In 2005, the first volume of the catalogue
raisonné was published. Ultimately, there will be five
volumes; every known Homer watercolor, drawing, and
oil will be listed and illustrated. The volumes are large
and handsome; they sell for $875 each. From the start
of this Homeric odyssey, Edith was Lloyd's assistant,
assembling descriptions of Homer's works, photos of
them, and precisely dated histories of exhibitions and
ownership. The work was sometimes tedious, but
mostly, Edith enjoyed it. One result of this joint effort
was that the Goodrichs became "the court of last resort"
concerning Homer's work: if they said a picture wasn't
authentic, that was that. Talk of newly discovered,
genuine Homers—and Homer fakes—was a dinnertime
staple for me. Fakes were annoying. Lloyd and Edith
became particularly irate when works they'd already
negated reappeared on the market. An especially
memorable oil showed two fishermen in a dory without
oars. "Winslow Homer," Lloyd told me emphatically,
"would never, *ever* send fishermen out to sea without
oars."

That Homer record keeping is remarkable, but what's even more extraordinary is that Lloyd and Edith also produced equally exhaustive, definitive records of the works of two more great American artists, Thomas Eakins and Albert Ryder. Ultimately, the Philadelphia Museum of Art and the library of the University of Delaware received those archives. They are visited frequently by authors, experts, and scholars, and catalogues will be published someday. That's something to be proud of—building bridges that lead into the future.

Three

SAKONNET

As if having Lloyd and Edith as parents wasn't luck enough, I spent my summers in Sakonnet.

That's the Indian name for Little Compton, a lovely, unspoiled Rhode Island coastal town squeezed up against the Massachusetts border. Population three thousand in winter, forty-five hundred in summer. Some of the summer people are rich, Social Register WASPs. The natives—farmers, fishermen, landscapers, blue-and white-collar workers—are Yankees or the descendants of Portuguese immigrants. A pocket-sized harbor full of small yachts and fishing and lobster boats; five miles inland, a picture-postcard village center: half a dozen wooden houses, a grade school, a general store, a small restaurant, a bank the size of a two-car garage, a Catholic church, and a white-painted, classically simple Congregational church with a steeple towering so high it can be seen from miles out at sea. Fishermen's nets are spread on fields for mending. Cows stare moronically over God-knows-how-many miles of stone walls. Barn-sized outcroppings of pink granite guard sandy beaches. Some of the trees shading the narrow, twisty roads bend permanently away from the prevailing southwest breeze. Thanks to the ocean dampness, paper clips leave rust stains. Beyond the green cornfields and meadows is the blue, gleaming Atlantic.

I was first taken to Sakonnet when I was ten months old. In Paris, there's a street called Gît le Coeur—"Here Lies the Heart." I've always felt that way about Sakonnet. When I was a little kid, if I had trouble getting to sleep, Edith would rub my back and say, "Think about Sakonnet;" as I drifted off, I'd be smiling, because that meant freedom (no school), and being "boiled" by white, thundering waves, and sitting high up on the rail of a heeling sailboat, and riding my bike to meet my friends. "It's so beautiful"—that's what people say, the first time they see Sakonnet. Everything there is on the right scale—there are no canyons, no redwoods, no warehouses, no railroad tracks. Little Compton is truly little. A century ago, it was a farming community, sending tons of potatoes, chickens, and geese to city markets. All my life, I've had the same nightmare: I long to go to Sakonnet, but when I arrive, the gorgeous landscape has been scarred and the modest, good-looking New England buildings have swollen hideously. Lloyd and Edith are buried in the Union cemetery, close to family and friends; my wife Patty and I own a plot there. Ever since I started writing, I've drawn Sakonnet in words as background, often to happy endings.

* * *

Sakonnet's first white resident was Benjamin Church, a thirty-three-year-old carpenter from Duxbury, Massachusetts; he arrived in 1674, planning to, in his words, "settle a new plantation where nothing was brought to; no preparation of dwelling house, or outhousing or fencing made. Horses and cattle were to be provided, ground to be cleared and broken up; the uttermost caution to be used, to keep myself free from offending my Indian neighbors." The Indians were several hundred Sakonnets, led by a female sachem, Awashonks. Church befriended her, and when the slaughter of King Phillip's War erupted, her warriors fought as the white men's allies. The young carpenter turned out to be a fierce leader, and his Sakonnets killed King Phillip.

The first white woman born in New England (in Plymouth, Massachusetts) was Betty Alden, the daughter of John and Priscilla. After marrying William Pabodie, she moved to Sakonnet around 1681. She lived to be ninety-four, at which point she had eighty-two grandchildren and five hundred and fifty-six great-grandchildren. Her descendants include Henry Wadsworth Longfellow, Adlai Stevenson, Orson Wells, and Marilyn Monroe (born Norma Jean Baker).

In the old burial ground is a stone saying, "Lidia, ye wife of Mr. Simeon Palmer who died December ye 26th 1754." Beside it is another stone saying, "Here lies Elizabeth who should have been the wife of Simeon Palmer." According to a local historian, during Lidia and Simeon's marriage, he "insisted on using cats for food." Lidia reluctantly played along. After she died (did she choke on a hairball?), Simeon married Elizabeth, who soon "rebelled and went home to her parents." After *she* died, "suddenly of a fever," Simeon chose her epitaph "so that all the world would know that this disobedient woman was not a proper wife."

The same local historian had a story about a 18th-century Little Compton character named "Butter Tom" Wilbour:

> It seems that Butter Tom's housekeeper lost her earrings and after hours of search gave them up for lost. The next day, Butter Tom, who was famous for his beard, combed out the hirsute adornment and the earrings dropped on the floor.

* * *

My grandfather, Henry Wickes Goodrich, started spending summers in Little Compton around 1900 (since most people now use that name for the place, I'll do so from now on). Getting there from Nutley wasn't easy. Lloyd said that "in addition to the five children and all the luggage, you had a household—a cook, a maid, a hired man, and a horse." The twenty-one-hour hegira was supervised by Lloyd's mother: Henry didn't care for confusion, so he made the trip a week later in solitary comfort. Step one was an Erie Railroad afternoon train to Hoboken; then came a ferry ride across the Hudson River. Hansom cabs, with the Goodrich horse fastened on behind, took them to the boat which carried them overnight to Fall River, Massachusetts. Then there was another train to Tiverton, Rhode Island, and finally two-horse, four-seated wagons transported them thirteen miles south to Little Compton—where friends welcomed them with strawberry shortcake.

For several summers, Henry rented; then he bought a handsome, eight-bedroom house with white columns across the front and a cupola on top. As a child, I spent many nights there, and was enchanted; I was sleeping in a palace! There was a good-sized barn, a two-story corncrib converted into a summer cottage, and meadows all around. All of this was close to three beaches, Sakonnet Harbor, and the brand-new Sakonnet Golf Club, which had a nine-hole course, a few tennis courts, and a clubhouse that had once been a farmhouse.

All his life, Lloyd loved Little Compton—and the feeling was particularly strong when we was a boy. "I remember," he once wrote to Edith, "when we used to come home in the fall, how I used to feel like weeping on the slightest provocation, from homesickness for the fields and the water, and how I used to bury myself in a book to forget about it."

One night when Lloyd was a boy, the stable caught on fire. The horse was rescued, but there was a danger that sparks might ignite the house's roof, because the volunteer firemen could wet only part of it. Then someone remembered that the two elderly, unmarried Cowan sisters, who lived across the road, had just bought a garden hose—a novelty in those days. They were on their verandah in their nightgowns, watching the excitement. A fireman ran to them—and they said, "We don't lend our garden hose" (the house came through okay).

Henry Goodrich's rich, Socialist brother-in-law, Henry Demarest Lloyd, visited Little Compton in 1889 and fell in love, buying thirty-two acres at the very end of Sakonnet Point: green meadows, a small, rocky hill overlooking a pond, and a long, sandy beach. In 1893, he built the biggest house in Little Compton, a handsome, shingled, three-story mansion with fifteen bedrooms that sat on the hill. He named it Watch House; there was a constant flow of guests, including his famous friends. His Communist sister Caro wrote that the front door was nine feet wide, "typifying the house's breadth of hospitality." The view was spectacular: to the east, Martha's Vineyard; to the west, Newport and its—Caro's words again—"marble palaces, homes reared on the proceeds of tyranny." On the mantel was a piece of driftwood on which Henry Lloyd wrote

> House on the Rock, where none shall knock,
> House on the Hill, I enter at will,
> House by the Sea, it harboreth me.
> House of the Rock, of the Hill, of the Sea,
> Maker and Master, hold watch over thee.

When Henry Demarest Lloyd was pacing on his long porch, savoring the sea air, he could see, roughly half a mile offshore, a three-acre outcropping of pinkish granite with half a dozen buildings on it and, at one end, a cliff towering higher than Watch House itself. This was West Island; the buildings housed an all-male club, opened in 1865, whose thirty members were mostly rich New Yorkers with names like Milbank, Schuyler, Van Rensselear, and Vanderbilt. The attraction (apart from money cozying up to money) was fishing for striped bass. Two of the most undistinguished U.S. presidents—Chester Arthur and Grover Cleveland—visited the club. There was a billiard room and a lounge; the food and drink were plentiful and top-drawer; members could bring their wives; some brought their valets. It was, everyone agreed, "capital fun."

About a quarter of a mile north of West Island was Sakonnet Lighthouse; the residents there—two male keepers—had no fun at all. The sixty-five-foot-tall, spark plug–shaped structure was built by the federal government on a low, slippery rock scarcely bigger than a baseball diamond, nine years after the fishing club. Getting on and off the rock was always perilous, and impossible in rough weather. The rock was confining, giving the keepers no room to stretch their legs. On three-acre West Island, there was room to walk around, and an area of soil where the staff grew vegetables and kept hens and a cow; on the rock, not a single plant grew. Obviously, the logical, infinitely more comfortable place to put the lighthouse was on top of West Island's highest cliff. So why didn't that happen? Well, the lighthouse flashed a bright signal (three short reds and a long white) all night long. Also, its foghorn, which could moan for hours, was very loud. All of that would've troubled the club members' sleep. Many Little Comptonites were convinced that strings had been pulled; in 1950, one of them wrote

I had a next-door neighbor who said, "Did you ever hear about President Arthur coming to visit on West Island?" It seems that he had arrived in a large, white naval vessel. "And when he left," she said, "after he had been wined and dined he had signed a piece of paper agreeing to put the lighthouse out on a lonely rock."

* * *

Caro loved Little Compton as much as her relations did, and around 1912, with three partners, she bought a one-hundred-and-thirty-two-acre farm. There were seven wells on the property plus a farmhouse and barn. The buyers got all this for $14,000—and soon sold the house and barn to a friend and many acres of land to the golf club. Caro kept the five-acre apple orchard and built a snug little cottage amid the ancient trees. She went there every summer, and when she wasn't writing articles for the *Daily Worker* or being visited by mustachioed, money-seeking Communists in black suits, she tended her garden. Describing her elderly, Portuguese gardener, she said, "He invariably begins any talk with me with an introductory expectoration, a kind of pulling himself together." Today I own Caro's house, and I wrote part of this book there.

In August 1924, my parents lived in a tent in Caro's orchard. They had a kerosene lamp; there was an outhouse nearby. One night, the tent blew down. "Well," Edith wrote, "that was a nor' easter! The skylight ripped off Caro's house, and the tent *flat* ... the lamp and mirror smashed and the books soaked. The bed and desk sticking up surrounded by overturned chairs and broken glass ... In the harbor, boats washed up on shore. The fishermen say they've lost all the money they made this summer."

Lloyd had to go to New York several times that summer; as in his childhood, he travelled on the Fall River Line's overnight boats. About one trip, he wrote to Edith:

> We had some aesthetic dancing, performed by a young man in faultless collegiate clothes, who was either crazy or very, very drunk ... In the rear of the main saloon, where everybody sits around and looks vacant, he did every known contortion, including oriental, classic, etc., all in time to the radio. The aged New England couples were fascinated.

(Until I was six, I also travelled to Sakonnet on Fall River Line boats. I particularly loved the flagship, the *Priscilla*, a four-hundred-and-forty-foot long, gleaming white steamer launched in 1893, capable of twenty-one miles per hour. This was luxury: carpeted decks, ornamental carvings, double-decker berths with sides to keep you from falling out in bad weather. The boats had a naughty reputation—married men took their "nieces" on overnight trips—and I once won sixty cents on a nickel slot machine. The best parts were watching the enormous, thumping, water-flinging side paddles— just like on a Mississippi River steamboat!—and eating supper outdoors on the topmost deck while rounding lower Manhattan: the sunset, the city skyline, the Statue of Liberty ...)

Lloyd and Edith built a simple, shingled, unheated four-bedroom summer house in Caro's orchard around the time I was born (1930). When they moved in, there were no town water or sewage systems (there still aren't); every family had its own well and septic tank. Everyone burned trash in open incinerators. The telephone system was primitive. Some phones were on party lines. Lloyd and Edith had a private line; their number was Two-Seven-One. To call a certain friend, I would say, "Two, please" to the operator.

In 1930, Prohibition was still in force. Ships from Canada would lie offshore; when bad weather kept the Coast Guard from patrolling, Sakonnet fishing and lobstering boats brought cases of liquor in, and men and boys took them to inland hiding places, sometimes under hay in farm wagons. The local people liked Prohibition, not because they disapproved of liquor, but because Prohibition provided work in a rural town where jobs were scarce. There was an ugly side to this: people who objected were threatened with bodily harm or the burning of their houses or barns and the poisoning of their wells. One night, when Lloyd was in New York, Edith heard gunfire, and saw tracer bullets flying over the water half a mile away; a Coast Guard boat was chasing a rum-runner. An hour later, in bed, she heard someone running toward the house. The running stopped and she heard panting—the man was sitting on the front stoop. After a minute, he got up and ran on.

The fishing club on West Island closed in 1906, and neglect, fire, and storms gradually destroyed the buildings. On the island's south side, there was a natural swimming pool that filled up at high tide; it was the perfect place for a picnic. Through the thirties and forties, Lloyd and Edith went often with friends. Sometimes, the picnickers stripped to go swimming; then, still nude, sipped drinks, ate lunch, and sketched and photographed each other.

Among the artists who visited Lloyd and Edith were the well-known, Japanese-born Yasuo Kuniyoshi and his wife, Katherine Schmidt, also a painter. Yas had pronunciation problems. On his first visit, he said, "Royd, I fought you riv in *Rong* Irlan, not *Lode* Irlan." Reg Marsh's father built a house overlooking Sakonnet

Harbor. When the Beach Club put up raw pine bathhouses, Reg decorated the interior walls of the Goodrichs' with funny, almost-life-sized pencil drawings of muscular dandies and buxom bathing beauties, using knotholes as buttocks and breasts. Instantly, that became the bathhouse everyone wanted to use.

An early houseguest of Lloyd and Edith's was John Gould Fletcher, an Arkansas-born, Pulitzer Prize–winning poet. He moved between the U.S. and England, and was occasionally hospitalized because of depression. He visited Little Compton in 1931, and it meant a lot to him: "I wish I were in your cottage," he wrote. "You do not know how good the days were ... Take a matchbox, fill it with Sakonnet sand, and send it to me post-post-haste ... I want to remember that there was *one* place I enjoyed in America." The "cottage" boasted a weathervane depicting a swordfish; when he left, Fletcher gave Lloyd and Edith a poem titled *Swordfish Weathervane*, which started, "Over the rooftop leaping / Out of the skies' blue-whiteness / Black against white, with sickle fins ..." In 1950, Fletcher lost his battle with depression, and drowned himself in a cattle pond in Little Rock.

Another poet Lloyd and Edith got to know well was Oliver Herford (1863-1935). Herford illustrated his own books of poems, satires, and magazine pieces. He'd been born in England, and as an adult wore a monocle and high, starched collars. The wisecracks, "My wife has a whim of iron" and "A woman's mind is cleaner than a man's because she changes it oftener" were attributed to him. The Goodrichs also spent time with the English-born essayist-novelist-biographer Llewelyn Powys, the brother of the writers John Cowper Powys and T. F. Powys. According to Edith, Llewelyn thought "shit" was one of the greatest words in the English language. She said he used to say, "'Shit.' It's so expressive, so perfect! 'Shit.'"

Oliver Herford had an equally clever, eccentric sister—Beatrice—a monologist who was praised by George Bernard Shaw and Alexander Woollcott ("If there is a more entertaining woman extant, someone has been concealing her from us"). Beatrice performed in vaudeville and on Broadway, imitating prattling train passengers, gabby boarding-house lodgers, or the kind of brat and scatterbrained mother "whose heads it would be a pleasure to crack together." As a kid, I saw Beatrice perform several times in Caro's Little Compton living room; she was magical. She grew flowers, and in winter left her straw gardening hat in her house "for the mice to sleep in." Not far away lived gay, Boston-born, Harvard-educated Harry Gardner, who bicycled everywhere. He had designed his own tiny, one-bedroom dwelling—"Minim"—and would suddenly pull built-in shelves and tables down from the walls in unexpected places; Beatrice called them "death-dealing breadboards." Beside Beatrice's house was a gazebo where she served afternoon tea. Her rich husband was crazy; his pockets were sewn closed so he couldn't hide knives, and a male keeper was constantly at his elbow. There was a fan-shaped window in the gazebo's rear wall. You'd be sipping tea, and suddenly Sidney's mad eyes would be glaring at you through the fan. Beatrice thought it was hilarious.

* * *

In November 1936, a Columbia University English professor invited a group of sixty- to ninety-year-old Little Compton natives to a meeting at the home of a local lady, and asked them to talk about the town's history. A microphone was hidden in a lamp; the professor wanted to preserve examples of pure New England speech for posterity. The recording showed that Little Comptonites used "help-keeper" for housekeeper and "scholar" for pupil; and pronounced shore "showa," hardly "hahly," cross-legged "krasligged," and large "lodge," One of the men there was eighty-four-year-old Abel Simmons, famous for an appearance in court in a dispute over water rights: when a lawyer asked him, "And have you lived in Little Compton all your life?" he replied, "Not yet."

That professor wasn't the only academic attracted to Little Compton. Some years later, the presidents of Vassar, Colgate, the University of New Hampshire, and Brown summered there simultaneously—in fact, there were *two* Brown presidents, one active and one retired. The retiree was named Barnaby Keeney. He was the first man to appear on the beach wearing a European-style swimsuit, and from then on, he was called Barney Bikini.

* * *

Sakonnet Harbor is a small, round cove with a skimpy breakwater protecting its north-facing entrance. On Tuesday, September 20, 1938, fishing and lobstering boats and a few pleasure boats rode at their moorings. Two fishing companies unloaded their catch onto good-sized docks. Strung along the harbor's low, sandy edge was a little fishing village: lodging houses and shanties, icehouses, boat and net houses, a few vacation cottages, and a fish market. A restaurant, The Fo'c's'le, had a barroom, a dance floor, and bowling alleys, and served "shore dinners"—steamed clams, chowder, fish, lobster. A store, Mack's, sold postcards, souvenirs, and two things I really loved: hot-buttered popcorn and ice cream; attached to it was a three-chair barbershop right out of a Norman Rockwell painting. The village was the scene of bustling activity, a place with a history; the word "picturesque" was often used.

On September 21, the 1938 Hurricane hit Sakonnet Point. Five fishermen drowned; every single building was carried away; the fishing docks were stripped down to bare pilings; only a handful of boats were left at their moorings. Many said that the village had been "swept away by a giant hand"—and the cliché was dead right.

The 1938 Hurricane was one of the worst disasters in New England history. In the state of Rhode Island, more than four hundred people were killed. It struck Little Compton incredibly hard; those who were there talked about it forever after. By far the most tragic event was, of course, the loss of the five fishermen. No one in Little Compton now knows their exact names— possibly because they were temporary workers, not town residents. They were evidently all living in the same building, and chose to stay put even when the wind strengthened in midday. In late afternoon, three gigantic waves swept over Sakonnet Point; there seems to be no record of where the bodies were found.

The most vivid description of the hurricane came from William Durfee, one of the keepers of Sakonnet Lighthouse, which stood right in the storm's path on its low, lonely rock:

> ... from twelve to two o'clock, the sea began to pound the station with a terrible force. The sky had an amber color ... By three o'clock, the wind blew a gale and the sea began to go higher and higher ... At five o'clock, all outside doors had been carried away and all windows were stove in, so that we were flooded practically out of our home ... I went into the tower to light it up. While there we took what was called the tidal wave. Three seas completely buried the sixty-six-foot-tall tower. The first sea broke seven deck plates out of the upper deck ... when it hit, it sounded like a cannon. And it hit with such force

as to knock me off my feet ... I must say
that neither I or Mr. Bouley ... were afraid
or considered ourselves in any danger ...
once in a while when an extra heavy sea
hit the tower Mr. Bouley would say, "Well,
I guess that one means business, it don't
seem to be taking any fooling" ... at three
a.m. I turned into a bed that was still
taking water ... At sunrise, Mr. Bouley
and I were surprised when we looked at
Sakonnet Point and saw that everything
had been washed away.

* * *

I was in Lloyd and Edith's house—my house—on
the day of the hurricane. I was eight; Lloyd was in
Boston, giving a lecture. I stood by a window, staring,
and, apart from the fact that Edith cried out every time
a tree came crashing down, I thought it was grand
entertainment. The next day, I wasn't so sure: an *awful
lot* of our trees were destroyed; there was sea water
right up to our gate; there was this terrible story about
five fishermen. For days, fallen trees blocked the roads;
people who walked to the shore found nightmarish
rubble; from the wreckage of The Fo'c's'le, I retrieved a
shattered bowling ball.

World War II didn't smite Little Compton as hard
as the 1938 Hurricane, but it did bring changes. To
protect the naval base at Newport, the Army installed
batteries of six-inch, eight-inch, and sixteen-inch guns
near the shore. Many acres were commandeered, and
huge emplacements and ammunition storage bunkers
went up. The barracks, officers' quarters, mess halls,
sentry boxes, headquarters, even the PX, were
constructed in "New England style"; the brilliant idea
was that the Germans, from their submarines, would
think they were looking at one vast farm. Appropriately,

all of this was named Fort Church. After the war, the military editor of *The New York Times,* Hanson Baldwin, told me that Fort Church, with all its firepower and barracks that looked like barns, was "already obsolete the day they started planning it."

Hundreds of GIs came to build Fort Church; and until the end of the war, around six hundred were stationed there—which is a lot, considering the town's size. My allowance bought low-priced candy bars at the PX. We went to the primitive little movie theater, which showed a new flick almost every night. Young girls were constantly nagged, "Be careful around the soldiers" (nothing ever happened). In fascination, from a mile away, we watched the test-firing of the sixteen-inchers. A long, pale gray cannon would poke slowly up out of its hole in the ground like a stiffened snake; gunnery calculations brought a pause; then there was a flame ball, then a monstrous bang, and then we could actually see the two-thousand-pound projectile's dark, pointed shape overhead as it soared toward a target twenty-five miles out at sea.

A teenaged-looking Coast Guard "Captain of the Fort" occasionally visited Sakonnet Harbor, which was active again, five years after the hurricane: the docks were repaired, and The Fo'c's'le and the fish market were rebuilt (but the rest of the little village was gone forever). Lloyd owned a fourteen-foot-long sailing dory (aboard which Reg Marsh had sprinkled my head with "gull droppings"). It was barely seaworthy, but we had to have documents: "Purpose of departure, pleasure ... No cameras, firearms, or binoculars allowed on board ... Navigation during the hours of darkness is prohibited ..."

* * *

Sakonnet Harbor's swordfishing boats had long bowsprits with stands on the end, where the harpooners—the "strikers"—did their job, and masts carrying high-up seats, for spotting the fish. When he was around ten, a friend of mine, Dudley, liked visiting the docks to watch the fishermen unloading the broad-billed catch. One fish made the day profitable; two meant living well for a week.

One afternoon, Dudley shyly asked if he could go out the next day.

The skipper was amused: "You want to see how it's done? Okay, but we leave at four-thirty AM. Get yourself here by then, or we'll be gone."

On his bicycle, Dudley arrived early and eager. By six AM, miles offshore, the skipper and crew were staring like Ahab over the calm sea, longing to see a sickle-shaped dorsal fin. The hours dragged by. There were dozen of sharks, but no swordfish. In early afternoon, the boat headed for home in deep gloom. Suddenly, Dudley pointed and cried in his high, little-boy voice, "What's that?" Thirty minutes later, a good-sized swordfish had been boated. The homeward voyage recommenced more cheerfully. Dudley pointed again. "What's *that*?" On the dock, after dressing out and weighing the two big prizes, the skipper said to Dudley, "Be sure you're ready tomorrow at four-thirty, when we pick you up."

My first fifteen summers in Little Compton were The Bicycle Years; the second fifteen were The Automobile Years (in Rhode Island, you got your driver's license at age sixteen).

Everything a kid under sixteen could possibly want was within bicycling distance of my house: the beach, the Golf Club, and the harbor, where one of the fishing docks had become the Sakonnet Yacht Club. The clubhouse consisted of (and still does) one large room where members stored sailing gear and squabbled after races about alleged infractions of the rules. The dues were minimal—as they were at the Beach Club and the

Golf Club; although there were rich families in Little Compton, everyone tried to keep everything simple. The Yacht Club's first steward was a gray-haired, Nova-Scotia-born retired fisherman named Tom, who had strong opinions, including "Readin' rots the mind." Tom had an unmarried sister. A story said that, years ago, Tom had been enraged when a "no-good Greek fisherman" jilted his sister, and the jilter's house burned down, with him inside. Another fisherman, Bill, when referring to a psychiatrist Yacht Club member, pronounced it "sick-a-trist"; his favorite cusswords were "Sweet American Jesus!" Bill had a nephew in his mid-thirties who delivered groceries for the general store. One day, a summer resident came home and found her house denuded of sheets, towels, silverware, dresses, and jewels. A month later, the police arrested Bill's nephew and recovered the loot in an apartment in Providence, which the nephew shared with two other gays. All three had been wearing the dresses on festive evenings and sleeping on the sheets; from prison, the thief wrote to the victim, "I'm sorry. We chose you because when I made deliveries to you, I really admired your taste."

The famous yacht designer and sailor, John Alden—I believe he's the only man ever to win three Bermuda races in boats he designed himself—was a summer Resident, and created a boat for local racing and day-sailing. The Sakonnet One-Design was handsome, sturdy, and eighteen feet long, with a large cockpit and a heavy keel (to handle the strong winds off Sakonnet Point). Over the years, roughly thirty were built; time and storms reduced the fleet; by 2008, only seven remained. In weekend races in my teens and twenties, I sometimes crewed for Mr. Alden. We won often, but crewing was complicated: in his later years, Mr. Alden was overweight and slow-moving; after he brought the boat about, we had to heave him by the belt from the leeward side up to the windward side. During one race, Mr. Alden spotted a tiny speck of sail way off on the horizon, and said something like "That's *Frisky*, a yawl I designed for Joe Jones thirty years ago." The other kid who was crewing with me whispered, "Nobody could identify a boat at that distance." Two hours later, *Frisky* sailed into Sakonnet Harbor. I also crewed for an elderly, eminent, highly competitive New York lawyer who sometimes broke the rules. When he got away with it, he'd say, "I shouldn't have done that. It's against my principles."

Much of Sakonnet's shoreline is rocky, but there are some sandy stretches. One of the prettiest—perhaps a fifth of a mile long—belongs to the Beach Club, where good-sized waves roll in. At one end, there's a West Island–like granite cliff, with diving boards; going off the highest takes nerve. The 1938 Hurricane smashed up the bathhouses; when the wreckage was reassembled, Reg Marsh's drawings wound up in several different ones: a beauty's left breast was here, her right breast was there. Instantly, *those* were the bathhouses everyone wanted to use. One year, two friends and I made a deal with the Beach Club: for a medium-generous sum, we would rake up and cart away all the seaweed that might come ashore that summer. This was great: honest labor, a season in the sun—and the possibility of more cash on the side: we'd been told that farmers were hungering for seaweed to use as fertilizer. The mountains of stinking weed that the tide deposited that August broke all records, and almost broke our backs. The farmers said, "Sure, we'll take that stuff—for free. Just spread it evenly between the rows of plants." We dumped the weed elsewhere.

I rode my bike to the Golf Club until I was sixteen, often wondering, "Today, will I caddy, or play?" The course was pleasant and unchallenging, with sparkling views out to sea ("Keep swimming long enough, and you'll hit Portugal"). I was never a good golfer, but I enjoyed it—and I also liked caddying: three hours of carrying two bags got you four dollars. Caddying was democratic: member's sons and local boys did it; we all got smacked with the same length of rubber hose when we misbehaved. The man with the hose was the golf pro, who (I now realize) was a bit crazy. His main source of income was golf lessons, but he also sold golf balls, tees, and candy bars out of a counter in the pro shop. If a caddy put his hand on the thick glass top, the hose crashed down, with the pro screaming, "Getcha greasy fingers offa there!" The pro's equally odd uncle was head greenskeeper. When my grandfather died, he told my father, "I always liked the old bastid."

Every summer, three dances were held in a good-sized club building with a stage inside; they were my introduction to nightlife glamour. The band, imported from Boston, was good; the girls wore their best dresses; the boys wore their best blazers and ties; many of the grownups gussied themselves up in evening dresses and white dinner jackets. Almost everyone smoked, and you had to know just how to cup a match in your hand against the breeze when lighting your date's coffin nail. As in similar summer colonies in those days, there were almost no Jews among the dancers (Lloyd and Edith helped to start breaking that down when they introduced New York friends into the community). One adult club member was famous for saying, "There are three ways to make money—earn it, marry it, and inherit it—and I've done them all." Another was accident-prone in strange ways. One summer, he had stomach pains; his doctor found a tick in his navel. During a trip to Germany, he needed to find a men's room in a restaurant. He didn't speak German. One door was marked "Herren;" that, he concluded, meant

"Hers." The other door said "Damen;" obviously, that meant "The Men," so in he went.

The club served no alcohol, but adult members could bring bottles to the dances, and drinks were mixed by club employees. On those nights, late-teenagers could bring beer. Some nights were warm, with a breeze that smelled of the ocean. When you weren't dancing you sat, your nose tender from the afternoon sun, on the long porch with a girl, looking at the stars while Cole Porter tunes, and voices, and laughter, drifted about. At midnight, someone passed the hat, hiring the band for another half-hour. Then kids would drive to the silent, closed-up Beach Club and climb out onto the big cliff, where the boys would dare the girls to jump off the highest board in their evening gowns. As they sprinted to the board's end, then hung magically suspended, then dropped toward the water, the girls screamed and tried (and failed) to keep their skirts from flying up over their faces. One of the gamest girls was Elvy, who was going to a fancy finishing school in Switzerland. Elvy's mother liked telling about a spring day when, discovering she had no butter in her Boston kitchen, and no cash, she redeemed some empty bottles at a local store. Back at home, she found a letter written by Elvy, at school, saying that for Easter she was going to Provence to visit a countess.

* * *

Rereading this chapter up to here, I realize I've made Sakonnet sound almost idyllic: golden sunshine, foamy white waves, lads and lasses at play, with only a few smudges on the record. In fact, like every other small town, the community has had truly dark moments.

Some Little Compton families owned slaves, who on Sundays were crowded into a small gallery in the Congregational church. In the summer of 1843, abolitionists insisted that the minister preach against slavery, but he refused: "It is not for us as a congregation to approve slavery or disapprove it. What has all this to do with preaching the Word of God?" (Happily, the minister soon resigned.)

The very next year, 1844, the social reformer Dorothea Dix visited Little Compton to rescue an insane man who was being held in a dungeon in the town poorhouse. The man, who sometimes "screamed dreadfully," was chained to the ceiling of his six-foot-square cell. "The place was filthy and damp," Dix wrote, "and the inmate stood near the door, motionless and silent, his tangled hair about his shoulders; his bare feet pressed the wet stone floor; he was emaciated, and more resembled a disinterred corpse than any living creature." There was already a small hospital for the insane in Providence; Dix told her Little Compton story to one of its sponsors, and the Providence facility was soon enlarged and improved (and, presumably, the Little Compton man was taken there).

In April 1964, my cousin Frances Hall visited her parents in Little Compton. An 18-year-old babysitter named Anne was hired to take care of the three Hall children, ages two to eight, while the adults were out. After dark—around 9:00—a twenty-year-old named Bobby, who had recently been discharged from the Army for "mental disability," knocked on the kitchen door. Concerned about the children, Anne went outside. Somehow, Bobby persuaded her to get into his truck. Exactly what happened there is unclear. In the end, Bobby struck Anne on the head with a rock, killing her. He then dragged her body into a nearby marsh, and fled. He was later found guilty of murder and sent to prison.

* * *

My Bicycle Years ended in 1946. My friends and I started driving twenty miles to an amusement park where we rode the roller coaster, and to a movie theater—like the rest of Ft. Church, the Army theater had closed at the end of the war. Now, before delivering your date home, you could drive her to a secluded spot—where, thanks to the code of the day, things leading up to It happened, but It never happened. In our later teens, we gathered for parties where a quartet of splendid-looking girls would join their virginal voices in *The Iceman's Song*: "Oh, lady, ice today, / Lady, it's nice today, / How 'bout a little piece today?" The girls glowed with the health that wealth, and tennis, and sun can bring, their tones were sweet and sure—and we boys thought, "Yeah, well, how *'bout* it?" (When they were feeling especially naughty, the girls sang a number which went, "Violate me in the violet time / In the vilest way that is known / Rape me and ravish me, utterly savage me / Let there be no mercy be shown.")

An advantage of the Automobile Years was, I could drive from one fishing spot to another, which improved my chances of catching striped bass. We used to cast into the surf for them, using bamboo poles and tricky reels; if you didn't control the line properly with your thumb, you lost precious minutes untangling a backlash. The fish sometimes sent spray flying as they fed; in heavy surf, you'd see them silhouetted like submarines in the wall of a wave. It was thrilling to have one strike, and play it, and land it. We caught fish weighing ten, fifteen, and twenty pounds; I once landed a thirty-eight-pounder. One day, I'd promised to meet a girl I was half in love with at a bus station when she arrived for the weekend. Stripers started jumping in front of me, their tails flashing, schools of the tiny silver fish they were chasing exploding out of the water. This was heaven! I landed one bass, then another—and then I realized I might be late. Burning with frustration, I threw the fish into the trunk compartment and cursed my feelings for the girl as I drove away.

After the Automobile Years came trains, planes, and ocean liners—but I often think I liked the Bicycle Years best.

Four

"WE GO FORTH UNAFRAID"

"Dalton—isn't that where the kids kick the teachers?"

In the 1930s and '40s, that question was asked more than once about the progressive school I was sent to from age two through fourteen. The answer is, No, that didn't happen—but there *was* a day when a teacher said, as a third-grader determinedly poured several bags of marbles out of a seventh-floor classroom window onto startled pedestrians on East Eight-Ninth Street, "We won't stop him. He's expressing himself."

That occurred shortly before Christmas. Years before, it had been decided that Dalton parents (many of whom were rich) would give their children toys, dolls, crayons, etc. to take to school, to be given to less fortunate kids; the marbles were part of that annual conscience payment. During the holiday season, Dalton had another ritual: an elaborately staged Christmas pageant featuring wings, halos, golden crowns, and a student choir singing Olde English carols. It required weeks of rehearsal, and every parent was expected to show up. I found the whole business odd because roughly two-thirds of the pupils and their parents were Jewish. My strongest pageant memory happened at age thirteen, when I played Joseph. I got the part because I was the second-tallest boy in the eighth grade; the tallest boy had the measles. Playing opposite me as Mary was beautiful Marian Seldes, today one of the country's finest actresses, a Tony winner, and a member of the Theatre Hall of Fame. I often wonder why, among her credits, she doesn't include, "Dalton School Christmas pageant, opposite David Goodrich."

Dalton has always attracted attention. When I was there, it was called "a haven for the children of professionals in the arts; intellectuals; affluent, successful German Jews; and WASPs interested in progressive education." Later, *Time* magazine said it was "the most progressive of the city's chic schools, and the most chic of the city's progressive schools ... it lets children set their own pace through a curriculum rich in art and music." In 1987, *Vanity Fair* magazine said that a Dalton child had written an essay starting, "We live in a large apartment. We are very poor. My mother is poor. My father is poor. Our maid is poor, our cook is poor, and my father's driver doesn't have any money at all." More flattering descriptions of the school include, "an educational model," "famous for its philosophy and historically rich in people and programs," and "internationally recognized for its academic excellence." My luck at Dalton was having gifted, sensitive teachers; growing up in an atmosphere of liberty and creativity; and being encouraged to ask questions, not to accept beliefs just because others did. The title of the school song is *We Go Forth Unafraid*.

* * *

The Dalton School was created by Miss Helen Parkhurst and Mrs. W. Murray Crane. Parkhurst, a grade school teacher, got interested in progressive education in the early 1900s, when educators began to question the tradition of drill and memorization and regimentation, and to believe that developing "the whole child" was important: children should learn to get along with others while enriching body, spirit, and mind.

Parkhurst developed what she called the Laboratory Plan, which had three elements: the House, where students were organized into small communities; the Laboratory, where they met individually with teachers; and the Assignment, individually planned studies for each student. She urged teachers to observe closely. "Have you ever watched a small child at a wash basin?" she once asked. "He doesn't wash his hands; he washes the soap."

Around 1915, Crane, the rich wife of the owner of the Crane Paper Company, hired Parkhurst to come to Dalton, Massachusetts, to supervise her daughter's education. Parkhurst briefly tried the Laboratory Plan in Dalton's public high school; in 1919, Crane helped her to open a grade school in the West Seventies, in New York; it was later named for the town, and the Laboratory Plan became the Dalton Plan. In 1922, Parkhurst published a book describing the Dalton Plan, which was translated into many languages; there are Dalton Schools in England, the Netherlands, and Japan. In 1929, the school moved into the building it occupies today, on East Eighty-Ninth Street; I started going there three years later.

Helen Parkhurst cared passionately about freedom for children and was a creative, forceful leader, but she was also authoritarian and paternalistic; her critics called her a despot. When pupils saw her coming, the atmosphere cooled; my sister Maddy almost got thrown out because at age seven, she stuck her tongue out at her. A teacher said that once, Parkhurst saw a boy facing the wrong direction in the Christmas pageant, picked him up by the hair, and turned him around. (This person said that Parkhurst appeared to be "sort of a gray mass ... gray hair ... She dressed gray. Everything seemed gray—but tremendous presence! Hypnotic eyes.") Parkhurst spent the school's money cavalierly— sometimes, it was said, on herself. She was adept at fundraising; reportedly, she gave several different parents the "exclusive" privilege of paying for an iron fence in front of the school.

In 1942, Dalton had to declare bankruptcy. This was rough on Parkhurst. She'd hired an expert to spot problems in children by examining their finger-painting. One day, to relax, she went alone to the art studio and did some dabbling. At a faculty meeting, not knowing who the finger-painter was, the expert held up the work and announced, "Here's a child who's deeply disturbed." Ultimately, Parkhurst was forced to resign, but she didn't leave quietly; she begged students to tell their parents, "I'm good, I really am." Lloyd was then secretary of the Board of Trustees; he helped with the school's financial reorganization.

* * *

Despite Parkhurst's despotism, she attracted a colorful, talented faculty, replete with prima donnas, who were dedicated to the humanistic liberal arts tradition. Few had graduate degrees; some had never taught before. One of them wrote—about being hired by Parkhurst to teach history—"I was not properly qualified to teach anything." This woman turned out to be a faculty mainstay and wrote five history books for children. Another history teacher, Mrs. Mukerji, reportedly joined the staff when she brought her four-year-old son in, hoping he'd be admitted on scholarship. The child looked around and said, "I like this place. I think I'll stay." He then leapt up into a chair and announced. "I am God and I just borned the whole world." Parkhurst accepted the boy. Thinking that his mother must be special because she allowed him so much freedom, Parkhurst asked her, "What do you do?" Mrs. Mujerki replied, "I'm planning to teach. I was educated at Stanford"; she was hired instantly. I recall vividly a fifth-grade Greek Festival organized by Mrs.

Mukerji: we all wore papier mâché helmets, and carried cardboard shields and wooden spears; some lucky kids got to ride in a chariot—but pulling the thing was okay too: you got to prance like a horse. Mrs. Mukerji's handsome Indian husband also taught history, and occasionally made the younger students observe periods of silence, saying, "If you're tranquil enough, you'll *hear* the silence." "It was quite enjoyable," one female graduate said. "There was a boy named Angus—very tall and silent. Very strange. He would periodically faint when we were listening to the silence, with a loud *thump*. We'd all say, 'There goes Angus again.' They would cart him out and the silence would continue."

Dalton teachers didn't give exams or marks; instead, they commented close-up: "*This* is good," "You can do better than *this*." The idea was to encourage individuality, to work intimately, to create a family feeling. "I still can't parse a sentence," another woman graduate said. "I was never taught 'this is a noun, this is a verb,' but I do believe I know how to use the English language ... My cousin went to a traditional school ... when we were in fifth grade, our parents were discussing education. My mother turned to my cousin and said, 'Would you do the six tables?' She started, 'Six times one, six times two,' and rapidly got to six times six, and stopped. She said, 'We haven't gone any further.' Then they called on me ... I began very laboriously figuring it out until I got to six times twelve ... I had been taught the tools and she had been taught by rote ... It's a perfect example of what the Dalton education is all about."

For several years, the well-known, Mexican-born artist Rufino Tamayo taught painting to the middle schoolers. (At the time, Dalton was divided into nursery school, kindergarten, middle school, and the all-girls high school; boys weren't taken into the high school until 1966.) "Mr. Tomato," as we called him behind his back, was handsome and temperamental; I'm sure he greatly preferred working in his studio to coping with children. His favorite, Mexican-accented words of instruction were, "Make it *larsh* (large)!" One of my best friends, Steve, used to sharpen his pencil to a needle point, then, in the corner of an enormous sheet of paper, make tiny, intricate drawings of imaginary machines. This drove Tamayo crazy, and we heard lots of "*Larsh! Larsh!*"—until one day Steve yelled back, "Make it larsh yourself, Mr. Tomato!" Another time, Tamayo did something totally un-Dalton-like. Seeing one little girl pushing another at a drinking fountain, he dragged the offender into the girls' bathroom, sat on one the child-sized toilets, threw her over his knee, and spanked her. (Tamayo had come to New York because doors were closed to him in Mexico: his paintings weren't revolutionary, like those of Rivera, Orozco, and Siqueiros. Ultimately, his paintings brought him international recognition. In 1981, a million-dollar museum bearing his name was built in Mexico City; some called it "Tamayo's Revenge.")

Tamayo never really got close to us, but another art teacher made us part of her life. Gwen Davies was ebullient and explosive, a Tallulah Bankhead in charm and sexiness; she threw herself around the room, calling everyone "Darling" and flourishing brushes. She wore heavy makeup and often had a cigarette dangling (the teachers weren't supposed to smoke in front of the children). She was born in England, and studied painting and singing in Paris; her vocal specialty was "the French Art Song," whatever that is. Another much-loved, English-born smoker was Harold Thorne, always called "Thornie." Dalton had a good-sized theater and emphasized the performing arts; in his cavernous backstage workshop, Thornie produced miracles of costume and scenery. The place smelled of cigarettes, paint, and glue, and the power saw made your ears

ring. Thornie was a joker; a student once saw him swat
Helen Parkhurst on the ass. He loved telling about a
sixth-grade historical play, which had twenty-six scenes:
"It was grand, with half the lines being ad-libbed, and I
never knew when to pull the curtain ... The opposing
armies had six men each and there was heavy slaughter—
and no curtain. Finally, about ten corpses cried out to
me, "Thornie, the curtain, *the curtain!*"

Our French teacher looked like a female Charles
de Gaulle: tall, long-nosed, aristocratic. Her accent was
impeccable. I learned to imitate it and ever since, when
I utter my inadequate French, people say, "You speak
well," and start talking twice as fast, which leaves me
totally lost. Our English teacher, Miss Dora Downes,
was (again!) born in England. She looked like a
Gainsborough—soft, brown hair, gray eyes, a straight,
perfect nose. She had a warm laugh and was much
loved, but gave an impression of correctitude, even
primness. People were surprised when she returned to
England in her sixties and got married; the idea of
Miss Downes waking to find a man's head on the next
pillow was hard to grasp. For Miss Downes, I wrote
essays that weren't just "What I Did Last Summer," but
the product of research and interviews. One described
the Sargasso Sea; for another, I talked with a lawyer
who'd started his career in the District Attorney's office,
prosecuting criminals. I discovered that writing was
stimulating (and hard work), and I wanted to do more
of it. I also learned the Reporter's Rule: "Be aggressive.
You won't know the answer 'til you ask the question."
(I've decided that the craft of writing is like the craft of
shoemaking: whether it's a sandal-sized magazine article
or a brogan-sized book, you find promising material,
select the choicest parts, stitch them together, and then
polish them—again and again and again.) Of course, I
had Lloyd and Frances in mind. They were a stimulus—
but also unsettling: could I possibly achieve as much

as they had? I've known many children of prominent, extra-successful people—and often that background hasn't been an advantage, but a burden.

* * *

Dalton's ten-story home, on East Eighty-Ninth Street between Park and Lexington Avenues, looked sort of like an apartment building, but more welcoming. In the basement, there was a swimming pool, the scene of many happy hours. There was a large theater on the ground floor. Stairs and elevators rose past offices, classrooms, science labs, art rooms, music rooms, and more classrooms, to a gym and, on the roof, an open-air playground for the kindergartners. Each division of the school had its own floors, so we eighth-grade boys seldom saw the high school girls, who were far more interesting than our own female classmates. The high schoolers wore long-sleeved, neck-to-knee smocks to protect their dresses and curb jealousy about fancy clothes; the smocks were ultra-modest, but we boys knew there were blossoming mysteries underneath.

In the thirties and forties, Dalton was proud of its liberal tone. In music class, children of the well-to-do sang working men's songs; one went, "Drill, ye tarriers, drill / Drill, ye tarriers, drill, / Work all day / For the sugar in yer tay / Down behind the railway, / Drill, ye tarriers, drill." We were told that tarriers were Welch miners—which sounded correct. However, the same teacher told us that the "backs" in a Princeton football song ("And send the backs on 'round the end") were "players who carry the ball behind their backs"—plainly, she knew more about the proletariat than the Ivy League. We sang the *Communist Internationale*, and I can still recite some of the words. In spite of the liberal atmosphere, there were no black students in the middle school—none, not even a token. Sadly, that was the case at almost all New York private schools at the time

(Dalton has since changed its admissions policy drastically).

At Dalton, the attitude toward religion was curious. We were taught a lot about Greek, Roman, and Indian mythology, where there were enough gods to confuse a kid, but the teachers said almost nothing about the Christian God—or, more importantly, considering the Jewish majority, about Jehovah. Only a few of my Jewish classmates went to temple. As I recall, I went to only one *bar mitzvah*, a stunner in the Waldorf Astoria's Starlight Roof with Meyer Davis's orchestra and twenty tables seating ten each. The hero of the day was the joker who'd poured marbles out the classroom window years before.

Lloyd and Edith weren't churchgoers, but they felt I should know something about the Christian religion; since Dalton wasn't teaching me about it, around age five they enrolled me in the Sunday School of the Episcopal Church of the Heavenly Rest. Many of the parishioners were rich, so it was called "the Church of the Heavily Dressed." It was on Ninetieth Street and Fifth Avenue; Lloyd and Edith took me to a Sunday service, then left me in a room where a dozen kids were seated on little chairs. The teacher asked, "Has anyone here not been baptized?" I raised my hand. No other hands went up, and everyone stared at me. When Lloyd and Edith picked me up, I said "Never again," and they said, "Amen."

In first through eighth grade, we seemed to have psychological tests every day, run by a large, frizzy-haired woman with a limp. One alumna said, "She seemed crazy ... One of her tests we called 'the spitball test.' 'Do you like to throw spitballs?' And every year you'd make up a new answer." The same alumna recalled a time when "Everybody went up to the gym and had to lie down on the floor and pretend you were a grapefruit with all the stuff being squeezed out of you. Or a sandbag with all the sand trickling out." To further probe their subconscious, kids were asked to draw pictures of their parents and siblings. One little girl, who was actually the product of a happy, stable home, stirred up the probers with depictions of herself and her brother cowering under a bed while their father beat their mother with a stick.

At Dalton, sports started on the roof, in kindergarten: tag, hopscotch, relay races. When you graduated downward to the gym, there was dodgeball, a kind of reverse football: when you threw the ball, you didn't want someone to catch it; you hoped it would smack someone hard. In Central Park, we played baseball, usually one team of Daltonians against another, but sometimes a Dalton team against a more traditional, all-boys school. That was disastrous: our "coaches" were, in fact, math or science teachers. At basketball, the results were equally dismal. Dalton's attitude toward organized sports was accurately reflected in "Backs are players who run with the ball behind their backs."

When my pal Steve and I were around ten, his father—who'd played on the Yale varsity baseball team (and been in Skull and Bones)—decided that Dalton's athletic program wasn't rigorous enough, and arranged private boxing lessons for us. Steve's father, a Wall Streeter, was a difficult, unhappy man. He and Steve's mother were divorced. In his forties, he got hit by a squash ball and lost an eye. He collected antique coin banks depicting blacks in comic poses and sang anti-Semitic songs. In 1941, Steve's very pretty mother started living with Jacques, a handsome, young, French artist/ski instructor who—as a pilot in the Free French Air Force—ferried planes from Canada to England, was shot down twice, and won the Croix de Guerre. I recall Jacques not as a dashing figure, but as the owner of a horrible, tiny monkey that had a nasty habit of leaping onto your shoulder and biting your ear. The monkey loved twisting open jars of cold cream and eating the contents (he would then develop serious diarrhea).

Dalton has always had more than its share of celebrity parents. One of my classmates, Penelope, was the daughter of Florence Eldridge and Fredric Marsh; I recall seeing them sit through a ghastly performance of *The Taming of the Shrew* with admirable patience. (The productions in the all-girl high school were far better: in addition to Marian Seldes, the actresses included Barbara Bel Geddes and Frances Sternhagen.) Wallace Shawn, the son of *New Yorker* editor William Shawn, also went to Dalton. A woman graduate said that Wallace—who is now a writer-actor, best known for *My Dinner with André*—was "tiny." In a fifth-grade Greek Festival, "He was Socrates. He had a man's cane, which on him was like a shepherd's crook. He had this funny little voice ... and he would say, 'Why do you say that?' Socrates was asking questions."

When I was in kindergarten, one of the playmates I was keenest on was Sadja Stokowski, the daughter of Leopold, the flamboyant, white-bushy-haired conductor of the New York Philharmonic Orchestra, and Evangeline Johnson, a striking, beautifully dressed heiress and arts patron. In the early twenties, the city of Palm Beach decreed that women couldn't wear skimpy bathing suits in public, and Evangeline had leaflets printed in protest and scattered them over the beach from the cockpit of a plane she'd just learned to fly. She had a house in New Milford, Connecticut, where—at age six—I spent an unforgettable weekend with Sadja, who had a merry laugh and curly, blond hair. While I was there it snowed, a miracle to me—I'd never before seen snow in the country—and Mrs. Stokowski and the maestro presided as Sadja and I shared a warm, bubbly bath. Sadja graduated from Radcliffe, went to medical school, married and had two children, and moved to California.

A specialist in women's health, she has published two books; in her spare time, she heads a small-town mediation board, helping to resolve conflicts between—for example—neighbors with barking dogs. From her glamorous childhood to her active adulthood, Sadja's story unmistakably says "Dalton."

In the early 1940s, "new, foreign" kids—refugees—started showing up at Dalton. Blonde, skinny Eloise Elmhurst's English family sent her to live with a New York family to escape the bombing of London; Emil Oberholtzer was German. Mei-Mei Lin, the daughter of the Chinese writer Lin Yu-tang, was delicate and gorgeous. Then there was George Shieh; the rumor was, he was somehow related to Chiang Kai-shek. George was lightly built, and the fucked-up son of a famous psychoanalyst bullied him. George took it for a couple of weeks, then erupted one day in the boys' bathroom, attacking his tormentor in a storm of punches, kicks, and Oriental shrieks, and chasing him into a toilet stall.

The boys' bathroom looked out on the rear of an apartment building. We realized that a funny-looking woman kept showing up in her window, roughly twenty yards away, to watch us standing at our urinals—a Peeping Thomasina! One day, when her window was open and she wasn't there, we stole modeling clay from the art room, moulded maybe twenty golf-ball-sized gobs, and threw them. A few stuck to the outside of the window, but many flew inside, adhering to walls, chairs, tables, and lampshades. That ended the peeping.

There was a Dalton outpost in Vermont—a coed summer camp run by a science teacher and her female partner, the editor of a woman's magazine. At age nine, I hated leaving Sakonnet, but then came overnight pony hikes (six boys and girls and a counselor, riding Shetlands in the mountains, with cooking gear and sleeping bags in a pony cart). Once, we made fishing tackle, using sticks cut from shrubs, ponytail hairs, and hooks the counselor kept pinned to his hatband. We dug worms for bait and ate brook trout grilled over a campfire. We also went on overnight canoe trips. When we paddled out onto Lake Champlain, the wind was kicking up lake-sized whitecaps, which alarmed some of my fellow campers. I felt superior: *if those scare you,* I thought, *try Sakonnet whitecaps.* The camp had its own deep, icy brook, where everyone swam nude, and its own small lake, where we learned to capsize a canoe, spend a minute underneath it treading water and breathing the air trapped in its upside-down hull, then right it. There was a pine tree draped with campers' pet snakes: sometimes there'd be four or five of the shiny creatures twined among the boughs—it looked like Christmas. The last night, as a farewell salute, each camper put a candle on a block of wood and let it drift across the lake: a fleet of bobbing, flickering flames.

I lived only a block and a half away from Dalton, and could walk to school, which meant no boring bus trips. Lloyd's Whitney Museum salary was skimpy, so our apartment was small: a dining alcove, a living room, two bedrooms, a maid's room, and two bathrooms. The building had white-gloved doormen, but was far from luxurious. Phone calls came through an antique switchboard in the lobby; I loved watching the operator, fat Miss Keating, as she flicked switches with flying hands while puffing cigarettes. In the alley behind the building, knife-sharpeners set up their grindstones and yelled up to open windows, and Italians bellowed operatic arias and we threw down coins. On the ground floor, facing Lexington Avenue, there was an old-fashioned drugstore, complete with soda fountain dispensing egg creams. In those days of coal furnaces, you sometimes got a tiny, airborne cinder in your eye; the pharmacist, fatherly "Doctor" Schuster, peeled back your lid and removed the speck with a corner of his spotless handkerchief.

My pals and I passed weekend hours in the Eighty-Sixth Street movie palaces, and rode the wonderful Third Avenue El; what we glimpsed through second-story windows was sometimes as intriguing as a movie. On the cardboard box containing a pound of Land O Lakes butter, there's a smiling Indian maiden, kneeling and holding out an identical box of Land O Lakes butter. Slicing around three sides of the maiden's offering with a razor blade creates a flap. Fold the cardboard carefully, and when you lift the flap, the lady's naked knees peek out, looking just like breasts. Another example of little-boy wickedness: we called the avenues around us—going west—Thirst, Sickened, Turd, Laxative, Puke, Medicine, and Filth. With my buddies, I explored heavily German Yorkville, and went to the Polo Grounds and Ebbetts Field. A dedicated Dodgers fan, I was in the stands during a disorderly game that lasted twenty-eight innings, during which someone threw a pop bottle that hit outfielder Ducky Medwick in the groin.

Everyone my age remembers the day of Pearl Harbor. I went to Central Park with Lloyd and Edith; when we returned, the doorman said something dreadful had happened. The two-foot-high, wood-encased, two-knob Philco radio told us the news—which, in retrospect, was far less frightening than 9/11. The Pearl Harbor damage was worse, but you knew who the enemy and your friends were; today, half the world seems to hate us. In 1943-'44, Lloyd served as an air raid warden, standing on the roof of our apartment building during trial blackouts wearing a World War I steel helmet, with buckets of sand nearby to smother German incendiary bombs.

Speaking of bombs: as we all know, little boys can be cruel and destructive. In Little Compton, Steve and I painstakingly built six-inch-high villages out of shingles, then blew them up with firecrackers. With .22 rifles, we killed wild rabbits and threw their bodies into the woods. The excuse was, we were protecting our parents' wartime vegetable plots (Victory Gardens), but in fact we were venting youthful sadism (now, whenever I see a Little Compton rabbit, I bleed a little). In New York, we worked off our aggression by throwing things out of apartment windows. Normally, a wooden kitchen match, released head downwards, would strike the sidewalk and ignite with a startling pop. If you dropped a fistful of matches, pedestrians had fiery little explosions all around them. My friend Nick Wood used to fling raw eggs out the window, aiming for the *other side* of Madison Avenue; people would look straight up, and we could observe them in safety. Nick once filled his bathtub with water, started a tiny model motorboat circling around, then dropped in a "depth charge"—a giant firecracker. There was an underwater *thump*, and a geyser—and a triangular hole in the bottom of the tub; although we quickly opened the drain, most of the water flowed into the apartment below.

The commonest out-the-window missiles were water bombs, made from paper cups, paper bags, or rubber balloons. You didn't try to *hit* people, just startle them. Henry ("Buck") Zuckerman was a baby-faced daredevil. Wearing roller skates, he'd grab hold of the rear of a Lexington Avenue bus and let it pull him along, sometimes at frightening speed. One afternoon, when we were about twelve, he filled a triple-sized balloon in the bathroom of his fifteenth-floor penthouse, carried it out onto the terrace, and tossed it over the wall without looking down. Five minutes later, the doorbell rang, and we heard the maid exclaim, "Not again!" Peeking into the vestibule, we saw the maid, a policeman, and a soaking-wet, middle-aged woman. Mrs. Zuckerman, a blonde ex-actress, was summoned from her chaise longue, where she'd been reading a novel and eating chocolates. She told me to go home; I wasn't needed to deal with this. Henry ("Buck") Zuckerman later changed his name to Buck Henry, and became an actor and a highly praised screenwriter (notably for *The Graduate*). He has two droll Dalton memories. In one, a pale, shy little boy took off his plastic leg and leaned it against the wall before jumping into the pool and "swimming like a fish." (When I told Buck that I didn't remember any one-legged fellow students, he said evasively, "He was probably the only one.") Also, Buck's parents once visited friends in Connecticut, near where Helen Parkhurst had a vacation house, and saw her playing passionate roulette at an illegal gambling club. "My parents nearly took me out of the school," he said. In 1970, *The New York Times* called Buck "Hollywood's hottest writer" and asked if there was an embarrassing secret from his past. "Well, yes," he replied. "A double sex change. I know this sounds strange, but when I was an adolescent I had a sex change, and then I changed my mind—which is every woman's prerogative."

Speaking of screenwriters in Park Avenue apartments: after school I often visited Douglas Goldman, who had a younger brother named Robert (also at Dalton). Visiting could be perilous. Several times, their courtly, bowtie-wearing father led me to a small oil painting that he insisted was by Winslow Homer. "I bought it from a friend of Homer's," Mr. Goldman would say, his tone getting steadily angrier. "It has all the elements of a Homer, and it's signed, but your father says it's a fake! His opinion has made it worthless!" I never knew how to reply. Douglas once showed me the cook's shopping list. For homogenized milk, she'd written, "homo milk;" we thought that was uproarious. Years later, Douglas married wonderful Swiss Jannie and settled in Italy. Robert shortened his name to Bo, and wound up writing three Oscar-winning screenplays. Bo was stout, like his father, and was constantly chuckling; you had the feeling he was memorizing bits of conversation for future use. At one point, he and *his* wonderful wife, Mab, and their children lived in a village near the Hudson River. Mab had a shed built which was half Bo's office and half the children's pony's stable. To give the pony a view of the river, Mab cut out a window between the two spaces; Bo sometimes looked up from his labors to find the pony staring at him through the opening like Beatrice Herford's mad husband.

* * *

In the years following Helen Parkhurst's resignation, Dalton became a very different place, and had mixed luck with heads-of-school.

Charlotte Durham, who'd previously led the high school, took over from Parkhurst. She was intelligent and well-loved, and wasn't asked to innovate. When she retired, the trustees chose Jack Kittell, PhD. His tenure was brief: his health became a problem, and he wanted to go back to California.

In 1964 came Donald Barr, a Columbia University dean. The trustees and parents who ran Dalton then didn't really care about progressive education; their focus was on getting their children into top colleges. Examinations and marks had always been anathema, but Barr, a rigorous conservative, brought them to Dalton. "There is no substitute," he reportedly said, "for the lash of competition." He also said, about permissive parents, "The trouble with many children is that their fathers are mothers and their mothers are sisters." He ruled with a strong hand, and was good at getting parents to open their pockets. Dalton's size doubled, and show business types and people with sparkly new money lined up to enroll their offspring.

The 1960s were, of course, a time of turmoil; trying to curb unruliness, Barr took strong steps. He imposed a dress code: "A girl's hemline is not to be higher than one inch above the knee ... Dungarees are not permitted. Shoes, not sneakers, are to be worn ... *the permissible length of a boy's hair is a matter for the school authorities to decide.*" A teacher reported that a high school student once asked Barr about the hair code, and Barr replied, "Long hair is masturbatory self-glorification." ("Barr," the teacher commented, "had a big, smart-ass mouth.") The dress code angered some students ("We are treated as the cream of the crop of our generation ... and yet we don't know how to dress ourselves properly. This assumption also contradicts a school policy of 'freedom of mind.'"). Students regularly violated it; today it no longer exists.

Barr came down hard on drugs: students who used or sold them, on or off campus, could be expelled. This annoyed many parents, who didn't regard marijuana as dangerous and disliked the school's policy for "after hours" users. Barr supported the Vietnam War; before an anti-war protest, he decreed that students who missed classes would face Saturday detention. The school's increased size distressed many Daltonians: "A sense of camaraderie and intimacy has been lost."

All of this created controversy and tension, and Dalton's students, faculty, administrators, parents, and alumni split into pro- and anti-Barr factions. In early 1970, four middle school students were thrown out for smoking marijuana at home, and the anti-Barrs decided to force him to resign. One of their leaders was a trustee because he was the president of the PTA. To protect Barr, the *pro*-Barrs decided to vote the PTA man out of office.

My wife, Patty, and I were at the evening PTA meeting (our daughter, Adele, was in the seventh grade) when the two sides clashed. So many parents showed up

that the meeting had to be held in the gym. *Time*
magazine wrote:

> What do TV host David Susskind,
> *Commentary* magazine editor Norman
> Podhoretz, actor Eli Wallach, critic Alfred
> Kazin, cartoonist Jules Feiffer, and a covey
> of New York's richest lawyers and brokers
> have in common? For one thing, they all
> ... send their children to... Dalton ... For
> another, they have lately turned their
> intellectual ferocity to intramural school
> brawling.

"Brawling" was the right word. In that gym, I'd hurled
dodgeballs with all my strength, but those men and
women outdid me a thousandfold. The pro-Barrs
outnumbered the antis and were better organized. They
booed and hissed; they seized microphone cords; they
drummed their feet on the floor in berserk unison. The
antis were silenced, and it was agreed that PTA members
would be polled by mail concerning their anti-Barr
president. Then, *Time* reported, "the combatants almost
reeled to their chauffeured limousines parked outside."

The pro-Barrs won the poll and took over the board
of trustees. Barr was now in full control; but four years
later, he had a major disagreement with the trustees
and resigned. The main reason was finances: costs
needed cutting and budgets were in disarray. His demise
reminded some people of Parkhurst's: although this
time there were no hints of hanky-panky, money was at
the root of it.

Dalton was now large, competitive, and newsworthy;
its educational system was far more traditional than
before. What Dalton needed was a steadying hand, and
in early 1975, Gardner Dunnan, a Harvard-trained
school administrator, was hired. During his twenty-

three years, the school became more efficient, selective, and academically demanding. Meanwhile, the students continued to explore, and to make mischief, in typically Dalton ways. In 1969, a thirteen-year-old had shown that throwing things out of windows was still a thrill—but this time it was a homemade, four-pound yo-yo that travelled from the school's tenth floor almost to the ground, then spun all the way back up. ("It's not Lindbergh crossing the Atlantic," his brother commented, "but it's almost as important.") Now, in Dunnan's time, an eleven-year-old became the youngest bridge life master up until then, and another was ranked as a chess master at age fourteen. As at many other high schools, music, sex, and designer jeans were everywhere—but one year, the kids added another dimension: decorating their jackets with dozens of buttons naming their favorite bands and political candidates. Gardner Dunnan ignored this until one girl displayed a large button saying FELLATIO; he then decreed a cut-down on buttons (the student newspaper decried the headmaster's "irresponsible attitude toward freedom of expression"). Dunnan's censorious streak showed again when four thirteen-year-olds broke into two business computer systems and the FBI raided the school; some people chuckled, but Dunnan said that chuckling "exacerbates the problem of understanding the ethics involved." Around the same time, Dunnan censored a faculty art show by removing ten nude photos. And then, in 1997, like Donald Barr, Gardner Dunnan resigned amidst controversy and newspaper headlines. This time, the root of the problem wasn't *l'argent*, but *l'amour*: he was having an affair with a female teacher. About Dunnan, the moralist, we can say, quoting Shakespeare, "The wicked fire of lust ... melted him" (*The Merry Wives of Windsor*, Act II, Scene 1, line 60).

* * *

The progressive school ethos of the 1930s and '40s emphasized independence and individuality: "You're unique," "You can do anything you set your mind to," "Your creations are valuable." It was wonderful to grow up hearing that, but in the real world, self-reliance isn't enough: people need training and mentors. From Dalton on, I liked the idea of writing—but the school hadn't taught me to fully appreciate the value of disciplined guidance. Almost all accomplishments involve relying on "the system" to some degree. Only geniuses can make it totally on their own; the rest of us need help.

* * *

In the 1947 high school yearbook, the director of admissions, Chloe Binger, saluted the graduating seniors in true Daltonese: "Darling 1947, be warm, be gay, keep your eyes open, and don't ever get stuffy. The world will love you, and you'll never grow old."

* * *

Dalton kids used to run in and out of the building with total freedom—it was *home*, a place without doors. Since 9/11, uniformed security men have patrolled outside; inside, every student, teacher, and administrator has to show an identity card. Years ago, there were no black children at the school; today, you might think you were in a wonderful mini-United Nations. Dalton athletic teams used to be pathetic; now, they meet their opponents in uniforms that say "Dalton Tigers" (where in God's name did "Tigers" come from?). Back in the 1940s, the science lab at arts-oriented Dalton was a small room seemingly containing one Bunsen burner and one microscope. In the twenty-first century, Dalton appears to have gone mad for technology; according to a recent publication, one can see "sixth-grade students being introduced to historic and scientific principles through simulated excavations of Assyria and Greece, high school students participating in advanced astronomy simulation, and English students exploring the ideas of Shakespeare's *Macbeth* through online resources, including digitized scenes from the play by three different repertory companies."

That's a long way from cardboard shields and papier mâché helmets.

In a 1992 book, Susan F. Semel wrote,

> The Dalton Plan has undergone a transformation since the days of Parkhurst ... Size of school,conservatism of parents, society's emphasis upon credentials, and leadership's reluctance to swim against the educational tide ... mitigate against preserving the Dalton Plan...

Many school songs celebrate the institution's history, or its superior spirit, or the delights of undergraduate years; they turn the places into objects of worship. Dalton's song is different: it's gentler, more humane; it praises an environment and a way of thinking and feeling; it talks about future possibilities. Many things have changed at Dalton, but not the school song. Written by a member of the class of 1936, it goes,

> We go forth unafraid,
> Strong with love and strong with learning,
> New worlds will be made
> Where we set our beacons burning;
>
> For each child,
> Great and small,
> Is friendly with man and beast
> And world that holds them all.

We sing to you, this is our praise,
Flung like a banner over Dalton days.
This is the school we have worked in and made.
Here we have learned to go forth unafraid.

Five

"BUILDER AND MOTHER OF MEN"

I left Dalton full of the spirit of the school song: I was unafraid.

I should've been afraid.

Loomis, a boys-only boarding school, was like nothing I'd ever known—a total shock.

I was sure my luck had run out.

Loomis sat amid vast playing fields outside Windsor, Connecticut, a few miles north of Hartford. Dormitory living, teachers called masters and addressed as "Sir," mediocre food, compulsory sports, compulsory chapel, compulsory Latin, compulsory jacket and tie, bells ringing hourly, tests graded from A to F. The song here was one of the worshipful kind ("Loomis, builder and mother of men, / Strong may you ever be, / Joyous, true and triumphant, / Beautiful and free ..."), and the place was hellbent upon inspiring virtue. Each year, at commencement, the prize given to the most outstanding graduate recognized his "Industry, Loyalty, and Manliness."

I was terrified.

And unbelievably homesick.

During my first weeks, the homesickness was worst when I ran. In July, I'd suddenly developed chest pains due to a leaky lung. My doctor called it "spontaneous mediastinal emphysema," and traced it back to a childhood case of pneumonia. It wasn't serious, he said, and would soon go away (it did), but for a year I should avoid contact sports (like football). Since no Loomis boy could be left idle on fall afternoons, I was ordered to run laps around a wooden track stuck away behind one of the football fields. I was all alone; the autumn sky was gray; as my sneakered feet thumped the boards and my breath streamed out, I thought I would die.

Four years later, I was near the top of my class scholastically, an editor of the school paper, the holder of the best-paying student job on campus, and reasonably happy. And I'd come to know four exceptional adults whose stories were weirdly linked.

* * *

Loomis opened in 1914, financed by an 1870s trust created by five childless members of the Connecticut Loomis family. When I got there, in 1944, there were roughly three hundred and fifty students—two-thirds boarders, one-third day students—and thirty-seven teachers. The campus, centered around a Georgian-colonial-style quadrangle—five brick, limestone-trimmed dormitories, a dining hall, and an administration-and-classroom building—was handsome; there was energy in the air.

As far as I remember, Lloyd and Edith never consulted me about going to boarding school. I think they wanted me out of New York so I could get more outdoor activity (which, in fact, I craved) and be less dependent on them (and my homesickness showed how strong that dependence was). Also, they probably felt I needed more rigorous teaching. Progressive education was great, but at some point, I had to face the demands of the traditional academic world. I think they chose Loomis because there was nothing fancy about it. It did a first-class job of educating middle-class boys, without the snobbery found in some prep schools. The students cleaned their own rooms, shoveled snow off the walks, and served as dining-hall waiters; the atmosphere was one hundred percent democratic. John D. Rockefeller Jr. sent two of his sons—John D. III and Winthrop—to Loomis, presumably so they could experience life on a less rarefied plane.

I made good friends at Loomis. Bert—blond, curly haired, a fine athlete—was from Atlanta. When he wasn't laughing, he was searching: "What did Faulkner *really* mean by that?" Michel, the son of the head of the Romance Languages Department at Smith College, could mimic teachers dead-on, played piano and guitar, and was on the fencing team. Another fencer, Tom, used to ram his foil through the keyhole of his dorm room without checking to see if anyone one was outside; we approached his room cautiously. The classmate I was closest to was Nicholas Taylor Stanford. Nick was tall, blond, blue-eyed, and handsome—my mother called him "The Greek God." He'd grown up in New York; his parents were divorced; his father was the publisher of a yachting magazine. Nick was a passionate sailor; his classroom doodles were yacht designs. Later, the summer he was twenty, he sailed his father's twenty-three-foot sloop singlehanded from Connecticut to Nova Scotia and back.

Adolescent boys are—of course—consumed by sexual longings. Students at today's boarding schools, many of which are coed, have no trouble getting laid, but we had no such luck. Adolescent boys also speak their own language; for example, there was "Fuckin'-A-Douche-Bag!" (today, this would be "Absolutely!"). Assessing a girl's attractiveness, we—all of us virgins—hid our insecurity behind bravado: "I wouldn't kick her out of bed." What's more, adolescent boys enjoy tormenting their elders. A teacher named Brayton Atwater ("Bud") Porter was a prime target. The lyrics of a popular song went, "In a strange caravan / Lives a lady they call / The Gypsy." Mr. Porter, a bachelor, lived in an apartment in one of the dormitories. Students used to creep up to his closed door carrying tennis balls, lustily sing, "In a strange caravan / Lives a weird little man / Dub Retrop" ("Bud Porter," backwards), then fling the balls at the door and scamper away.

There was a pecking order at the school. Seniors had special privileges. A peer-elected student council handled some disciplinary problems, punishing malefactors with extra time in study hall. There were rules about almost everything: "Boys must wear hats and coats when they are out of doors in the winter." "In the dining hall, no table shall rise until one at which a master has been sitting has risen." "No one shall enter or leave a building through a window." The school also tried to govern off-campus behavior: "No student shall drink any alcoholic beverage, or have it purchased for him in a public place."

Athletes were much admired. One year, the baseball team was undefeated, with lopsided scores against Choate, Kent, Taft, Hotchkiss, and some other schools, thanks to an amazing pitcher named Frank Quinn, who sometimes struck out eighteen or twenty batters in a game. Quinn went to Yale; as a sophomore, he won seven games and lost none. He quit Yale early and the Boston Red Sox signed him. He soon faded. In my Loomis senior year, I saw him visiting the campus, looking cocky and drinking from a flask. Phil Isenberg, a class behind Quinn, was as good an athlete—captain of both the football and baseball teams (and first violinist of the school orchestra and president of the student council). He had a very different post-Loomis story; at Harvard, he was football captain; he later became a respected psychiatrist.

Because Lloyd's Whitney Museum salary was minimal, I had a scholarship. To earn extra money, I worked in the office that monitored student class attendance and off-campus visits during my junior and senior years. This could be awkward, because I was sometimes asked for favors. Like most minor bureaucrats, I tried to remain honest but occasionally obliged my friends. I may have learned as much in that job as in my classrooms.

I wrote news and feature pieces for the weekly, four-page newspaper, the *Loomis Log*, and in my junior year became number two on the editorial board. Each year, we gave the biggest headlines to the story reporting who'd be the editors next year. The *Log* accepted ads. Rogers Peet, the New York men's clothing store, ran a notice inviting Loomisites to submit copy for an ad to appear in an upcoming issue; the best would win a twenty-dollar gift certificate. I mailed in a submission and got a letter declaring me the winner. After collecting my prize from a store executive in New York, I asked how many other boys I'd beaten. With a smile he said, "Yours was the only entry." That shrank my pride—but never mind: I had proof that writing *could* pay. The literary magazine, *The Loom*, published a couple of my short stories and gave a prize to a poem of mine. I reread the poem recently, and am doing readers the kindness of not reprinting it here.

I'd always known you could scythe with a scythe, but at Dalton, the teachers hadn't told us anything about nouns and verbs—they'd just insisted that we write decent English. Now I had to learn new terminology; I also had to learn a new language, Latin (you had to take two years of it). One of the Latin teachers, who looked wise behind his beard, was named Knower Mills. Other teachers included Mr. Norris, called "Squirrel" because of his pouchy cheeks; Mr. Fowles, "Blue Lou" because of his five o'clock shadow; and Mr. Stookins, who'd studied at the Sorbonne and taught French. The athletic director, Mr. Erickson, was grotesque: glowering at you, he rubbed his chin with a hand that had no index finger.

Loomis had a "sister" school, Chaffee, which had its own campus nearby—roughly a hundred girls, all day students. We boarders saw them only at dances or when they performed in Loomis's small theater. I joined the Stagehands Union so I could meet these comely creatures. In addition to the theater, other buildings stood near the quadrangle: science labs, a gym, an infirmary, faculty houses, and a chapel. The handsomest building was the dining hall: over thirty round tables for ten, potted ferns, and a cork floor to deaden adolescent clatter. The ceiling was impressively high, but we discovered that if you folded one of the linen napkins into a narrow strip, let it dangle with a pat of butter in the middle, then snapped the two ends sharply outward, you could catapult the butter up there, and it would stick.

I came out of that long-ago New York Sunday school session turned off by churchgoing. At Loomis, attending chapel was mandatory. The services were bland Episcopalian. Grace—always, "Bless, Oh Lord, this food to our use, and us to Thyself in service"—was said before dining hall meals. I remained an agnostic, but I learned to love hymns: the thundering, growling organ music and the poetic words. Since then, at other church services, when hymns are sung, I repeat the words I learned at Loomis silently, to myself: I can't carry a tune, so I don't inflict my attempts on others.

The school was good at its essential job—preparing students for college. In my senior year, with my jacket neatly buttoned and my tie neatly knotted, I entered the office of the college placement counselor. The conversation was brief:

"Where do you want to go, Goodrich?"

"Yale, Sir."

"Done. Send in the next boy."

The dormitories had long, second-floor porches facing into the quadrangle; the bedrooms there were for seniors only. In the spring, you could sit out on the porch in a deck chair, gazing up at the splendid elms and down at the underclassmen. I recall thinking in May of '48, just before commencement, that I'd earned the contentment I was feeling—and I glowed with the knowledge that I'd soon be gone.

* * *

The first of the four exceptional Loomis adults I was exposed to was Nathaniel Horton Batchelder— Massachusetts-born (1880), Harvard-educated, tall, tweedy, and sturdily built, with a bulldog jaw and silver hair parted down the middle. Previously an English teacher at Hotchkiss, he'd become Loomis' first headmaster in 1914 at age thirty-four, and at age sixty-four he still had that job. In many ways, he'd *created* Loomis, studying similar institutions, hiring the architects, helping to plan the campus, hiring the faculty. He was a Yankee to the bone, a dynamo, a man with a boundless energy and a strong Puritan streak. He liked being called "Mister B" (it made him sound warm), and promoted himself as a loving father figure, but he had absolute dominion over the school, and could burst into ferocious shouting when displeased. This happened most often in the dining hall, when the noise level irked him: he shot up from his chair with his enormous lower mandible thrust forward and started bellowing: "*I will not have this! Do you hear me? Stop this instantly!*"

Total, cowed silence.

When he was thirty, Mr. B married Gwendolyn Sedgwick Mead; they had a son. She died in 1917, and Mr. B hired a sculptor named Evelyn Beatrice Longman to do a memorial portrait of her. As in a fairy tale, love blossomed, and in 1920, the headmaster and the sculptor were married. This second Mrs. Batchelder was the second remarkable adult I encountered at Loomis.

Mrs. B didn't *look* remarkable: gray-haired, short, plump, in her mid-sixties, she might have been anyone's mother. Her husband insisted that she serve as hostess in their large, formally furnished Headmaster's House, presiding at tea and playing Chinese checkers with groups of students; she was shy, so that seemed to be hard for her. Every year, the evening before the start of Christmas vacation, the entire student body gathered in the school library after dinner, and Mr. B read Dickens's *Christmas Carol* aloud. He wore a black suit; Mrs. B wore an evening gown and shiny jewels. They sat in armchairs before a fireplace glowing with "the Yule log;" some years (it's hard to believe), a student dressed in a jester's costume—tights, cap with bells— sat on the floor before them. In a powerful voice heard in every corner of the room, Mr. B would intone. We students were keyed up—tomorrow, vacation would start, we'd escape for two weeks! As Dickens's wonderful words rolled on, we held our breath, waiting for the description of Mr. and Mrs. Fezziwig dancing. "And when old Fezziwig and Mrs. Fezziwig had gone through all the dance," the headmaster read, "bow and curtsey; corkscrew; thread-the-needle, and back to your place, Fezziwig cut—cut so deftly, that he appeared to wink with his legs." To us, "to cut" was short for "to cut the cheese"—to fart. With those words, faces turned purple and chairs shook as we struggled to hold in laughter. Incredibly, the Batchelders never caught on, but younger masters did, and kept order with stern stares.

Mrs. Batchelder's ordinary looks were deceptive. Born poor in Ohio in 1874, she left school at fourteen, then worked in a dry goods store and saved enough money to study sculpture at the Chicago Art Institute. In New York, she became an assistant to one of the country's leading sculptors, Daniel Chester French. In 1904, she won a silver medal at the Louisiana Exposition, and her career took off. She created many monumental works, including bronze doors for the U.S. Naval Academy chapel and the Wellesley College library, and portraits of the presidents of Harvard and the University of Pennsylvania. Her best-known sculpture was "Golden Boy," the American Telephone and Telegraph Company's tall male figure wrapped in electric cables and holding lightning bolts; gilded, it stood atop the company's New York headquarters; a drawing of it appeared on telephone directories. She was the first woman sculptor elected to the National Academy of Design. She had an enormous studio on the Loomis campus built by her husband—no doubt with school money. She sold many pieces to the school: it seemed that everywhere you looked, there was a plaque commemorating a deceased teacher.

Every day after lunch, Mr. B clinked a spoon against his glass, rose, and read announcements: "Soccer practice is cancelled this afternoon;" "The French Club will meet at five." He sometimes summoned students to his table—which meant you were in deep trouble. One day, it happened to me. I approached trembling—but Mr. B merely said, "My wife would like to speak to you."

I sat beside her. "When was you last haircut?" she asked.

We were supposed to get shorn every two weeks; I quickly said, "I'm going to the barber tomorrow."

A smile. "Don't. I've spoken to your dorm master. He'll let you grow your hair for two more weeks. Then come to my studio."

At the time, Mrs. Batchelder was working on a life-sized memorial to Loomis boys killed in World War II—a nude male angel, complete with wings, bending over a nude, wounded warrior and offering him a cup of water. In her studio—it had a big skylight, and smelled of wet clay—Mrs. B sat me on a stool, dampened my hair with water, "sculpted" my hair with her fingers, then copied it onto the angel's clay head. After an hour, she thanked me in her tiny voice and shyly handed me a dollar bill—four times the cost of a haircut. The bronze statue, titled *The Victory of Mercy*, was unveiled in 1948; as of today, the angel's still wearing my hair. (A few years before, Mrs. B. used Arthur Ochs Sulzberger, now the publisher of *The New York Times*, as a model. He was evidently a poor student; about his modeling experience, his sister jokingly wrote, "Since he did not afford anyone the opportunity to judge what was inside his head, it was gratifying that the outside at least was admired.")

The third remarkable person I met at Loomis was the head of the English department, Norris Ely Orchard—sometimes called "Neo" thanks to his initials. Neo was in his mid-thirties, wispy, dark-haired, and a Phi Beta Kappa at Yale. He was also dapper, witty, and faintly effeminate. He was a first-rate teacher who had his finger in many extracurricular pies: the theatrical productions, *The Log*, and *The Loom*. Mr. Orchard wrote two plays, which he put on at Loomis—their titles, *Lady Agatha Walks Again* and *Acme Paper Doilies*, signaled his sexual orientation. He also wrote a bestselling "how to" book, *Study Successfully*, published by McGraw-Hill. Students liked him: at his dining hall table, we played a game where you spoke three consecutive letters, and if the other players didn't believe that the sequence could occur in an actual word, they challenged you. I still recall Mr. Orchard's glee when he announced that w-s-s shows up in "newsstand." He dressed conservatively and used to say, "If someone thinks you're well dressed, but a moment later can't remember what you were wearing, you *were* well dressed." His theatrical side showed when he entered a classroom. He'd start running outside, then—frozen in a pose on his leather heels like a performer on ice skates—he'd glide across the slickly polished wooden floor and come to a grinning halt at his desk.

On the very first day of my senior year, the fourth of my memorable Loomisites—an English teacher who'd recently been discharged from the Army—walked into the classroom, introduced himself as John Horne Burns, and silently wrote ten questions on the blackboard. Among them were, "What is a rune?" and "Who says 'Finalmente mia'?" and "What is the plant that screams?" He then said, "You have three minutes to answer. You won't be graded—this is just to show me if you're cultured." He collected our answer sheets, which were almost entirely blank, gave us our next-day assignment, and said there'd be a one-minute quiz then that *would* be graded.

"We'll do that every class," he said. "There'll be only one short question—and I guarantee you won't know the answer if you haven't done the reading. You are now dismissed."

We walked out in a daze. What kind of torture was this? Who was this guy? And what in God's name were the answers to those crazy questions? (Mr. Burns later told us: a rune is a Finnish or Old Norse poem; Scarpia, the villain in *Tosca*, says "Finalmente mia;" in *Romeo and Juliet*, one of the characters says, "And shrieks the mandrakes torn out of the earth.")

John Horne Burns was the best teacher I ever had anywhere, in anything. He was constantly asking for our opinions and challenging us. He welcomed our questions, and if he couldn't answer them, he'd say so, then answer the next day.. He'd started teaching at Loomis in 1937, right after Harvard (where he too had been Phi Beta Kappa). He was then drafted and admitted to Officer Candidate School, where he was almost thrown out for accidentally shooting a cow.

Commissioned as a second lieutenant, he served in
North Africa and Italy, interrogating prisoners of war
and censoring their mail (in his own words, he "sat
out" the war). He was average-sized with reddish hair,
a long nose, and a scar on his forehead caused by
forceps at birth. A non-practicing Catholic with three
younger brothers and three younger sisters, he was
born in Andover, Massachusetts, where he'd gone to
Phillips Academy. He played piano and organ, and had
been a soloist in the Harvard Glee Club. His smiles
were sardonic, as were his comments on the themes
we wrote. If he caught you faking it, he drew a little pile
of manure in the margin, with a shovel stuck in it.

If they had their parents' permission, seniors could
smoke in a master's apartment after dinner. Four other
boys and I visited Mr. Burns often, to light up, drink
coffee, and listen to opera records. He was funny and
stimulating, and seemed to welcome our company. We
were sure he was homosexual; he was careful not to do
or say anything that might confirm that. We knew that
he sometimes drank heavily—in the morning, he looked
hungover, and you could smell the booze. Some
evenings, while we smoked, he closed his bedroom door
and started typing. We knew that he'd produced eight
unpublished novels, four at Harvard and four while
teaching. That showed amazing discipline and
determination. "You know that I am stubborn enough,"
he wrote to a friend, "to find time for anything I want to
do ... little boys cannot joggle my pen, even if they peep
and pule over my shoulder." (Mr. Burns liked words
like "joggle" and "pule." I once said I didn't own a
thesaurus, and he advised me to buy one that was
"buckram bound.") His ninth novel, about his war
experiences, had just been published by Harper &
Brothers.

Mr. Burn's novel, *The Gallery*, consisted of a series
of alternating "Portraits" and "Promenades." The nine

Portraits described people involved in the Allied invasion of Italy, among them an AWOL GI with trench foot; the female, Italian owner of a gay bar; and a hard-line Baptist Army chaplain. The Promenades were actually one long, highly subjective commentary, written in the first person, dated progressively: Casablanca, Fedhala, Algiers, and Naples. All of the Portraits, and some of the Promenades, in some way involved a Neapolitan gathering-place that gave the book its title. The first paragraph of the book went

> There's an arcade in Naples that they call the Galleria Umberto Primo. It's a cross between a railroad station and a church. You think you're in a museum till you see the bars and the shops. Once this Galleria had a dome of glass, but the bombings of Naples shattered this sky-light, and tinkling glass fell like cruel snow to the pavement. But life went on in the Galleria. In August, 1944, it was the unofficial heart of Naples. It was a living and subdividing cell of vermouth, Allied soldiery, and the Italian people.

The Gallery has been forgotten today, but in 1947, it was a sensation. Authors would kill for the reviews it got: "A novel of extraordinary skill and power"; "There are passages which can only be described as 'terrific'"; "A new literary star has risen." Edmund Wilson, in *The New Yorker*, called it "remarkable." Some years later, Ernest Hemingway said, "The only truly good novel, maybe great, to come out of World War II is *The Gallery*," and Gore Vidal wrote, "Of the well-known books of the Second War, I have always thought that only Burns' account was authentic and felt ... For Burns the war was authentic revelation. In Naples he fell in

love with the idea of life." The book was filled with
compassion for both the conquered and the conquerors:
"There is a fervent sensitivity, a passionate sympathy,"
The New York Times' reviewer wrote, "in the writing ...
the author's concern for the living people—for their
fumbling, perilous attachments, and responsibilities
... is revealed."

For many Loomis boys, having a celebrated author
in our midst was thrilling. He signed our copies of *The
Gallery* with cheery messages; when our parents visited,
we introduced them (Edith asked Mr. Burns where he
found his characters, and with a grin he replied, "You
may be in my next book"). *The Gallery* sold well in
hardcover and paperback, and pleasing royalty checks
arrived. Reportedly, a movie company made a
substantial offer; reportedly, Mr. Burns turned it down
because the company wanted to use only part of the
book, and he wanted the whole thing filmed. He began
going to New York on long weekends, sometimes
missing Monday classes. He seemed distracted, and
plainly was drinking more. During a New York vacation,
I saw him at the opera, liquored-up, with an obviously
gay man. Then, in January '48, he disappeared, and
another teacher finished his courses. There were rumors
about a fight with Mr. B; we were sorry he'd gone.

* * *

It can happen: you think you know a person well;
you've got him/her figured out. And then that individual
does something totally unexpected. When John Horne
Burns' next novel was published, the people who'd
known him at Loomis got one hell of a jolt.

The hero of *Lucifer With a Book* (spring 1949)
was Burns himself, renamed Guy Hudson and
transformed into a tall, battle-hardened Army veteran
with a mouth turned up into a "permanent leer" by a
"terrible scar" ("A mortar shell exploded near me at

Malmedy. In December 1944"). Eager for honest work, Hudson has signed on as a history teacher at a boys' boarding school, The Academy, "a place of beauty and poise." He's a sardonic iconoclast; a student thinks he's "different from anybody on the faculty and has come back from the war against everything ... His cold, savage mastery is thrilling." Hudson is bisexual, and by the book's end has seduced a female Spanish teacher at The Academy's sister school. That affair and Hudson's opposition to a radical curriculum change constitute the plot; the rest of the book explores what a *New York Times* reviewer called Hudson's

> self-crucifixion, his ragged inner monologues... Guy Hudson finds he is doomed and damned from the first academic get-together ... He loathes every faculty member and most of the students ... and is cordially loathed in return. The focus of his hatred is the headmaster, a troglodyte... The final explosion comes when the headmaster decides to begin compulsory military training ... Guy, with thundering rhetoric, calls his employer a Fascist ... collects the Spanish teacher (who now loves him as only an awakened WAC captain can love) and departs in search of a school where junior history professors will be understood ...

Burns dashed off this three-hundred-and-forty-page tale in just seven months. What's most shocking is its savagery. *The Gallery* brimmed over with compassion; *Lucifer* exuded contempt. Apart from Guy Hudson and his WAC, there's hardly a character Burns doesn't despise. The *Times* reviewer said he'd created "a novel that hates its people and its locale passionately."

Burns' first target was the stentorian, authoritarian (but also creative, effective, and worthy) Mr. Batchelder, now called "Mr. Pilkey" and turned into a windbag and a fool. With students, Pilkey was "deliciously condescending." He never stopped talking: "his words kept coming in a wall of sound." He wasn't a barbarian; he just didn't go by any earthly code of etiquette. He "crammed down great mouthfuls of crisp pork ... snorting with gourmand happiness," then belched. He cheated at backgammon "like the craftiest child." At a faculty party, demonstrating his football punting, he accidentally kicked a tray of hors d'oeuvres, sending "shrimp and crackers and mayonnaise heavenward." The drunken faculty laughed, and "Guy Hudson had the same sensation he'd known in Berlin, seeing human beings and swine rooting for substance in the same rubble."

When Burns described Mrs. Batchelder, she wasn't a dignified, respected creator of monumental sculpture, but a twit who "spent her days in an attic painting designs on crockery ... Her brain was glazed from licking the tips of little brushes with which she stippled eagles and gryphons onto old china." At a faculty party, she cried out to a servant, "That pitcher of iced coffee is two inches off center!" She had false teeth that clicked and varicose veins that "throbbed," "clamored," and produced "nagging agony."

Burns saved his fiercest acid for Norris Orchard, whom he called "Philbrick Grimes." (In Evelyn Waugh's great satirical novel, *Decline and Fall*, two of the leading characters are a butler named Philbrick—an ex-criminal who talks about revolting crimes—and Captain Grimes, a comically incompetent teacher at an abysmal boys' boarding school who's both pederastic and a bigamist, and has "abominable features" and a wooden leg.) At the Academy, Philbrick Grimes has many extracurricular positions. He is "light on his feet" and "flutters like a hummingbird." At age thirteen, he "discovered how girls are different from boys," and "the shock closed his little brain to sex ... At age thirty seven he'd never known woman." He "skipped about his room much like a little girl taking inventory of her dollhouse." He hadn't been drafted because he'd been declared "MILDLY PSYCHOTIC—OLD BIDDY TYPE—EXTREME ANXIETY STATE—NOT TO BE INDUCTED FOR ANY REASON WHATSOEVER."

In addition to being venomous, *Lucifer* was, in many places, atrociously written. One sample, describing Guy Hudson's deflowering of the WAC captain, will suffice:

> He became an executioner, an avenging icepick against virgin ice. Crying aloud murderous and ravaging things, he reduced her beneath his hands and his lunging body to what she essentially was, to what she had come into the world to be. He drew her on like a glove ...

On second thought, that won't suffice. On the very next page, the lady was miraculously changed:

> And turning to her, as tender as before he'd been devilish, he taught her what love is like. She was indeed reborn. She joined him in all delights, surpassing him in invention and sensuality. Finally he was exhausted and lay weak and laughing beside her. For her mouth had said wild words he'd never expected to hear from her, and their excitement and climaxes were dual now.

* * *

What was it in John Horne Burns that made him spew bile so viciously in *Lucifer*? Was he always a hater?

Before *The Gallery*'s publication, Harper's asked for biographical information, and Burns wrote, "I live in a peculiar remove from life which makes me watch people as though they were swimming in an aquarium … I specialize in needling people … The only point I can offer in defense of myself is that I am as nasty with myself as I can be with others." He added that his mother had given him "the mercilessness that she used against herself and on all of her children." One of Burn's brothers, Tom, a successful Boston lawyer, told me that their mother was "an extremely difficult woman … Jack was our mother's *all* … There was always a smart-aleckness in Jack. He could be vicious in his attacks on people, which I'm sure he got from our mother, who was loaded with this sort of nastiness."

And Burns' hatred of Mr. B—where did that come from?

"The headmaster," Burns wrote to his Harper editor, "dealt me what I consider the meanest cut of my life, so I walked out." We don't know what the "meanest cut" was, but obviously the wound was deep. Also, it may be that Burns grew up hating all male authority figures. Tom Burns said that their mother was "dreadful" to their father: "How he ever stayed with her, I'll never know." Since John Horne Burns was extremely close to his mother, perhaps she passed down her detestation of "bosses."

Burns' treatment of Mrs. Batchelder was also shameful: he appreciated the arts, but viciously ridiculed a fellow-artist's professional accomplishments, meanwhile turning her into a fool.

Did Burns heap abuse onto Norris Orchard because Orchard, head of the English department, was another authority figure? More important may be the climate of that time. Almost all gays stayed in the closet then; having to live that way must have been agonizing—and anger-making; maybe Burns unloaded the fury he felt about the system onto Orchard. Or maybe Orchard represented a part of himself that he was ashamed of?

Finally, why did this keen judge of great literature write so many trashy paragraphs? Perhaps he was thinking, "I'm considered a genius; any book will be well received." Now without a job, he needed money; that pressure may have warped his judgment. Perhaps he loaded *Lucifer* with (absurd) sex in the hope that it would help sales. Naming a character Philbrick Grimes suggests that he was hoping to create an Evelyn Waugh-like satire—but he missed that target by many miles.

* * *

Nathaniel Horton Batchelder stepped down as headmaster in 1949. He and Mrs. B settled on Cape Cod, in Osterville, where they had a vacation house and another studio. She died there in 1954, he in 1956.

Norris Orchard also died on Cape Cod—in South Harwich. In late '55, he had two brain operations. The problem was never publicly described, but it was probably cancer. He went on leave, then returned briefly to teach, but then had to have further treatment. In March '57, he killed himself. A newspaper account makes heartbreaking reading:

> A search party found Mr. Orchard's body seated against a scrub pine about 1,000 yards from the home of his parents … death was the result of self-inflicted knife wounds in the wrists and neck … He had been despondent in recent weeks, feeling that he would become a burden to his parents.

John Horne Burns died before the Batchelders and Mr. Orchard. In a way, he was another suicide—and his story was also heartbreaking.

At first, after leaving Loomis, life was pleasant for Burns. He rented a five-room apartment in Boston's mostly Italian West End, and wrote to a friend that he drank "special Manhattans," ate lobster, loved to "analyze the grime of Boston," and hated to go to bed before dawn. He still wore his Army khakis and a weird-looking red corduroy hat. He worked hard on a new novel, and was thinking about a play "which I pray will put me up in Tennessee Williams's league." *Holiday* magazine sent him to Italy, North Africa, and Ireland to write eleven travel pieces, and paid him well. The year 1948, he told a friend, was crucial because it marked a turn toward "my lifelong ambition to support myself entirely by my pen (or typewriter)."

Then came devastating reviews of *Lucifer with a Book*: "ill-considered and immature," "too much of it consists of stereotypes and righteous indignation," "unpalatable and frequently tasteless," "Mr. Burns has dipped his pen too deeply in gall."

Burns' next novel, *A Cry of Children* (1952), told the story of a rich young concert pianist who leaves his bullying mother to marry a Boston Irish Catholic girl; when their passion fades, he takes up with a new virgin he finds singing sweetly in church. A few reviews were kind, but most were negative: "I failed to find anything particularly fresh or stirring," "It all has the standard overtones of America as the crushing mechanistic society." Burns himself wrote that it was "admired by practically no one." By then, he was living "in a chilly villa outside Florence, Italy" and was finishing his fourth novel, which would deal with "St. Francis of Assisi in modern life. If that novel is a fiasco I will take up gardening and write a book about that."

The move to Italy was sudden: "He just disappeared," his brother Tom said. "In Florence, he knew Bernard Berenson ... He taught at a university in Livorno ... An Italian bartender friend of his called him 'The Professor.'" That all sounds pleasant—but things weren't going well. Gore Vidal later wrote,

> He seemed to have lost some inner sense of self, gained in the war, lost in peace. He disintegrated. Night after night, he would stand at the Excelsior Hotel bar, drinking brandy ... insulting imagined enemies and imagined friends, and ... complaining of what had been done to him by book reviewers. In those years one tried not to think of Burns; it was too bitter.

The fourth novel, *The Stranger's Guise*, added to Burns' troubles. Although he said he'd "never written with such love and calm," an editor told him in July '53 that it needed extensive revision; a few days later, Harper's rejected it. In August, at age thirty-six, he slipped into a coma while sailing and died; a coroner concluded he had a sun-induced cerebral hemorrhage. There were rumors that he'd killed himself—he was said to have just ended a troubled affair with an Italian doctor—but Tom Burns is sure that the hemorrhage "came because of his drinking." He was buried in Rome, but Tom said, "Our mother wanted his body back ... He's buried in a Catholic cemetery outside Boston." To quote Gore Vidal again,

> Burns was a gifted man who wrote a book far in excess of his gift, making a kind of masterpiece which will endure in a way that he could not. Extreme circumstances

made him write a book which was better than his talent, an unbearable fate for an ambitious artist who wants to go on, but cannot ... I suspect that once Burns realized his situation, he in fact chose not to go on, and between Italian brandy and Italian sun, contrived to stop.

Six

"BOOLA-BOOLA"

Asked at Loomis which college I preferred, I said, "Yale." I'm not sure why; maybe because the graduates I knew loved the place. In fact, I knew almost nothing about it. I'd been there only once, when the son of some friends of Lloyd and Edith showed me around, then, during lunch at Mory's, warned me about a notorious sadist, the head of the athletic program: "He'll make you do painful, horribly embarrassing things."

That turned out to be an exaggeration—but not totally. To show that you were in decent physical shape, you swam briefly in the gymnasium pool, then did some basic exercises. The embarrassing part came when they took a photo of you, to study your posture. It felt humiliatingly like the police taking a "mug shot"—except you were naked, standing sideways to the camera, and the main feature of the photo wasn't your nose. It was rumored that new arrivals at women's colleges—maybe Smith, Vassar—were photographed in the same way, and copies of the photos were on sale somewhere; I suspect that was just wishful thinking.

When I walked onto the campus in September '48, I was awed by the ancient elms, the Gothic-style buildings, and the Ivy League ivy. My fellow students and the few professors I could identify as such led to further awe. The university, I decided, was far larger, handsomer, more impressive, and more challenging, than I'd expected.

Two days later—before I knew my way around, or how things worked, or *anything*—blind luck (there it is again) shaped my next four years. Like all scholarship ("bursary") students, I had to have a part-time job to cover my room and board. At the bursar's office, I was told that my main option was serving and cleaning up in dining halls—but there were also the student agencies, small companies the university had set up to provide certain services. If I wanted, I could talk to the agency people, and take a week to decide if I wanted to work for them. Otherwise, I'd start slinging hash tomorrow. In Little Compton, I'd told a girl that I hoped to return for an end-of-summer weekend; if I wasn't working in a dining hall, I could make the trip. "I'll check out the agencies," I said.

Amazingly, the first person I saw in the agency building was a Little Comptonite named Charlie. He was driving back for the weekend, and offered me a lift. "But," he said, "you shouldn't go. You should stay here and compete for a job with the Student Suit Pressing Agency."

It turned out that Charlie, a senior, was the president of the Student Suit Pressing Agency. They didn't do the actual cleaning and pressing; the key was, they were the only company allowed to pick up and deliver on campus. Other student-run agencies provided laundry service, sold Yale stationery, sold firewood, and so forth. The beauty, Charlie said, was that if an agency made a profit, the managers kept part of it. "Dining hall work proves nothing," he added. "Here, you learn something about running a small business, and you make some cash."

I hated giving up my Little Compton weekend—and at first I hated the competition I'd entered. Roughly twenty other freshmen were knocking on doors, trying to sign up customers; the top-selling five would be hired to collect the money owed and do various office tasks. In sophomore year, the two best performers would become the agency's managers.

Climbing up staircase after staircase, I started to learn Yale's geography: the Old Campus, the residential colleges, the law and graduate Schools. To my amazement, I found a line from a novel I'd loved as a ten-year-old—*Scaramouche,* by Rafael Sabatini— inscribed over a door in the Hall of Graduate Studies; it went, "Born with the gift of laughter and the sense that the world was mad" (the building's architect didn't like its Gothic style, and put the quote there as a joke). While selling suit-pressing services, I learned something about myself: I was competitive. At Dalton, the idea had been, "Cooperate with others." At Loomis, the rigid grading system meant that we worked for our teachers' approbation. Now, for the first time, I was in an honest-to-God race, and I decided to win.

Selling could be tricky. You'd knock on a door and say, "Hi. Can I interest you in ..." Most of the time, you were treated civilly. Sometimes there was exasperation: "You're the tenth salesman today!" And occasionally you'd get a response that meant, "Go away, you're my inferior, I look down upon you, go away."

That happened seldom, and of course no one ever used those exact words, but the impression was deep. These people were totally unlike anyone I'd met at Dalton or Loomis. They came from privileged backgrounds and ancient prep schools; they were arrogant; they felt entitled; they perpetuated an elitist, "Neath-the-Elms-of-Dear-Old-Yale" atmosphere. Their condescension wasn't aimed only at agency representatives; it also showed up in the places I'd avoided, the residential college dining halls. On September 30 of that year, the *Yale Daily News* ran an editorial saying,

There is increasing evidence of discourtesy and plain bad manners in the attitude toward the bursary students who help serve food and clean tables. It should be clear that these men are no one's servants; even if they were, it would be inexcusable to treat them with the disdain that has on occasion been noticeable.

Selling and collecting were hard work, but by my senior year, Forrest ("Woody") Grumney and I were running the agency. We paid ourselves a small salary, and in our last month split a satisfying bonus; Woody—brown crewcut, funny, from an Ohio high school—may have been the only undergraduate to send money home to his mother. His greatest joy was starring as shortstop on Yale's varsity baseball team.

When my class first got to New Haven, there were eleven-hundred and sixty of us. Roughly ten percent were ex-servicemen; roughly twenty-five percent were sons of alumni. Forty-eight percent had gone to private schools. As elsewhere in the Ivy League, there was a Jewish quota, and Catholics found themselves rooming with other Catholics. Our class had exactly four black men in it. Like all the other freshmen, they had sent photos with their applications. They'd been told by letter that they'd be assigned roommates at random—names would be drawn out of a hat. Fifty years later, one of them, Charles Benjamin Payne Jr., wrote

Somehow it didn't come as a surprise ... that my two roommates were also men of color ... It later transpired that the fourth Negro, as we were then called, was sufficiently fair to photograph white, and so was rooming with a freshman from Texas ... After comparing letters, we decided that Yale didn't lie—it just had several hats.

An aunt of Payne's had worked as a maid at Yale in the 1930s. In 1949, to show her that a member of her family had "made it," Payne invited her to his rooms. She was obviously proud of him, but in the bedroom, her expression suddenly showed—he later wrote—"panic and despair." It turned out that among the blankets he'd brought from home was one she'd stolen from a student's room in the '30s, then given to his mother. "Now it had returned," Payne wrote, and his aunt was afraid that the Yale authorities would "seek her out." Payne calmed his aunt and kept the blanket. After Yale, he got an MD and practiced in Cleveland; he also taught at four different institutions. In 1976, his daughter received a BA; they were the first African-American father-and-daughter team to graduate from Yale.

Yale's student-run radio station often played *Collegiate*, a song that glorified infantile hijinks ("Alpha, Beta, Lambda, Chi, Omega, / Delta handa poker,/ We're collegiate, rah, rah, rah!"). The station did this tongue in cheek, but in my day, Yalies *were* infantile in many ways. Footwear indicated social status: if you wore white buckskin shoes, you were "white shoe" (from an elite background); "black shoe" meant the opposite. *The* man to buy liquor from was Mort Rappaport ("See Mort for that snort, let Rappaport wrap that quart"). Mort's vodka was combined with grapefruit juice to make Seabreezes, which inexperienced revelers then threw up (I don't recall a single party where *someone* didn't throw up). Our dates came from women's colleges; their chastity was seldom threatened. The secret societies (like Skull and Bones) were taken seriously, and one night a week, as in a children's game, files of members in dark suits would parade across the campus, headed for their mausoleums; they didn't speak to one another or to anyone else. A Yale football coach once told his team, "Gentlemen, you are about to play football against Harvard. Never again in your lives will you do anything so important." In 1948, traces of that kind of foolishness still hung in the air.

In my first month at Yale, I had a one hundred percent collegiate experience. One Saturday night, I visited the bar of the DKE fraternity house (where America's worst-ever president, "George the Decider," was later a mainstay). When the place closed, four DKEs and I started driving to another bar. While passing a road construction barrier, two of them leaned out and pulled red warning lanterns into the car. Instantly, a police car appeared. Charged with petty larceny of city property, the five of us spent a thoroughly miserable night in jail. A month later, in a downtown courtroom, we hung our heads while a lawyer hired by the car's driver entered a plea of *nolo*. The judge quickly dismissed us—he was related to the best custom tailor in town, who made the driver's handsome jackets and trousers.

Yale students got their mail at a post office on the Old Campus. Occasionally, a weirdo named George Frederick Gundelfinger, an '03 graduate, mailed us warnings about "the Yale virus of license, lethargy, and bigotry." Our sex lives worried him: he had some vague theories about increasing mental strength through "sexual sublimation." One of his tracts was titled *The Penis Mightier Than the Sword*. He deplored what he called the Communist influence at Yale. When William F. Buckley published his career-starting book, *God and Man at Yale*, also alleging leftist tendencies on campus, some of us wondered if Buckley was a Gundelfinger acolyte.

Sylvia, the girl I didn't get to see in Little Compton, was in her senior year at stuffy Miss Porter's School, in Farmington, not far away. She might as well have been in a nunnery. She could have male visitors only on Saturday afternoons, for two hours. She and the men walked through the town only on certain streets, within sight of the headmaster's house. Then came tea with that humorless man and his wife, then a closely watched farewell handshake. I borrowed a car and drove there. During our walk, Sylvia complained nonstop about the school. When I'd left her and was walking toward the car, I spotted something shiny on the sidewalk: a pearl necklace. I picked it up and walked back; the headmaster answered his doorbell. I said, "I just found this." I'll never forget the look he gave me: obviously, I hadn't *found* the necklace, I'd brought it with me, and now I was trying to outwit him in some tricky way and corrupt his cloistered virgins. He took it silently from my hand and closed the door.

* * *

The class of '52 has been called one of Yale's least distinguished. We were part of the Silent Generation, and many of us worked only hard enough to earn a "gentleman's C," then unimaginatively joined Corporate America. A classmate wrote, "Almost without exception, we were inarticulate, we were detached, there was an absence of fury. Undergraduate life ... stagnated under our sway." I agree with that; still, some of us later accomplished a good deal; for example, one became Secretary of the Treasury, and another was U.S. Attorney for the Southern District of New York. I was on nodding terms with those individuals, but was closer to some other standouts.

John Bissell was gangly and sweet-natured. In the early sixties, he married a prominent Indian lady in New Delhi and started a successful company that exported locally made fabrics. In 1992, he founded a school for young girls in rural Rajasthan, where literacy was low among women (families sent only boys to

English-language schools). The school subsidized the students' tuition; it began with eleven students; by 2007, there were nearly six hundred.

Ed Hastings—a Loomis graduate and one of my Yale roommates—acted and produced Off Broadway, then helped to found the American Conservatory Theater, a highly praised, nonprofit, San Francisco-based performance and educational group, ultimately becoming artistic director. After retiring, he directed productions in China, Serbo-Croatia, and Russia.

Steve Larner, my Dalton pal whose drawings enraged Mr. Tomato, was my Yale classmate. He became a prize-winning cinematographer, shooting documentaries around the world and movies and TV shows in Hollywood. "I always sought out films," he wrote, "dealing with the human condition ... One such was *Roots*, from Alex Haley's novel, the first twelve-hour mini-series." After he retired, Steve and his wife started a vineyard in California. "Shooting films," he reported, "is like a walk in the park compared to vineyard work."

In freshman year, two hundred and forty '52-ites were housed in deteriorating Army barracks a mile from the campus. One resident regularly released his pet bat in a hallway "to exercise his wings." To demonstrate the flimsiness of the interior, beaverboard walls, students threw silver dollars through them. High school—as opposed to prep school—graduates seemed to have been disproportionately picked for these slums. Congenial, boyish-looking, extra-smart George Adams suffered through barracks life, then was on the editorial board of the *Yale Daily News*, edited the Senior Class Book, and was a member of a fraternity and one of the secret societies. He became a partner in a top-level New York law firm and for several years was head of the board of trustees of Sarah Lawrence College. He and his wife, Lucy, had three daughters and a son. The girls all went to Yale; the boy went to Sarah Lawrence.

As in previous years, in the 1950s Yale's secret societies chose new members mostly because they were rich, or socially prominent, or star jocks, or leaders in extracurricular activities. Courtly, German-born Colin Eisler was taken into Skull and Bones because of his undergraduate intellectual record. After getting a PhD, he taught art history, ultimately becoming a full professor at New York University. In 1991, Skull and Bones' undergraduates voted to admit women. Stuffy, older Bonesmen were outraged and actually changed the locks on their building, causing Colin to write to *The New York Times*, saying he was "mortified" and adding that he'd joined the club "in the folly of youth." and had hoped that when Yale went coed, "the senior societies would shrivel up and die, expecting women to have more sense and pride than to lend their presence to the mindless pomp of senior societies. Friendship by preselection and confidence by decree are wrong … None of the joys achieved … can equal the disappointment and exclusion they generate."

For twenty-three years after graduation, in business school and the Foreign Service, Bob DeVecchi (in his words) "kept hoping that something would come up that would challenge me to the core." In 1975, he joined the International Rescue Committee, a refugee relief organization. He ultimately became executive director. The job, he wrote, took him to "some of the best, and many of the worst, corners of the world … I have waded into … the Gulf of Siam to pull ashore a boatload of Vietnamese refugees. I have held a Cambodian baby in my arms as it drew its last faint breath … with flack jacket and helmet, I have dodged bullets in Sarajevo. I have become a … fixture in Washington—from the Situation Room at the White House, to the State Department …" In 2005, Yale recognized Bob's contributions by awarding him an honorary degree as Doctor of Humane Letters.

The class of '52 also included some unsuccessful—and strange—men. Earl wore costly clothes from J. Press (sometimes called "J. Squeeze"). During freshman year, two drinks would turn him violent and crazy—screaming curses, punching, even biting. My roommates and I couldn't talk him back to normal—and if we called the campus cops they'd lock him up—so we stripped him and held him under a cold shower. That worked—but Earl drank and went crazy several more times. Then one day, he just packed up and went home. Another guy, rigid, driven Bill, was intent on making a quick fortune. He married a rich Connecticut girl in sophomore year; I was an usher in his elaborate wedding. He sent a letter detailing what ushers should wear, including, "Shoes—black calf, highly polished; Hose—black silk, lisle, or nylon; Garters—yes." He too dropped out of Yale; five years later, I ran into him in New York and he borrowed two hundred dollars from me. I never saw him again.

To get to New York for a weekend, there was the train—but there was also a student name Richard M. Scaife, who drove undergraduates to midtown for less money. I rode with this driver-for-hire several times. It later emerged that his middle name was Mellon. Harvey O'Connor showed how Andrew Mellon, Scaife's great-uncle, worshipped money; plainly, that was in the DNA. Scaife flunked out of Yale, became an alcoholic, and pumped millions into conservative causes; he's been called "the man who funded the movement that made 'family values' a watchword of the right." In 2005, when Scaife was worth $1.4 billion, his second marriage broke up and his wife discovered he'd been taking his girlfriend to a motel that rented rooms for three hours for $31.

* * *

Compared to Loomis, much of my Yale classwork was easy. Because of the suit-pressing agency, I had few free hours; I spent them reading books not covered in my courses, and *The New Yorker*. I particularly admired John O'Hara's short stories and S. J. Perelman's humor pieces. Perelman was a friend of my parents', and in 1949 inscribed a copy of one of his travel books, "To Lloyd, this highly prejudiced and deplorably illiterate narrative of escapism, rascality, and double dealing, from its remorseless progenitor." Years later, at Frances and Albert's dinner parties, I got to know Perelman; like many professional humorists, he was often silent and depressed. Because she was the youngest, most attractive woman there, the Hacketts often seated my wife, Patty, next to Perelman. Patty struggled to get him talking, but finally found the magic words: "Have you done any interesting travelling recently?" Thereafter, she had a hard time shutting him up.

My major, American Studies, allowed me to choose courses freely, so I got to hear some terrific professors.

Under the leadership of Henri Peyre, Yale's Department of Romance Languages was ranked first in the U.S. several times by the American Council on Education. I took Peyre's basic French literature course, and I agree with the student who wrote, "The educational value sometimes becomes so great that it cannot be purchased with the debased currency of the ordinary mind." Peyre was a quintessential Frenchman: "The only sport I enjoy is conversing with women. Most of life is a purely nuance affair, and women help men realize this. Yale is much too masculine a place."

Cleanth Brooks wrote or edited some thirty books, most notably *The Well-Wrought Urn*, which argued that what was important about understanding a poem wasn't the background of its author or the work's cultural setting, but its inner meaning and structure. Brooks was diffident and scholarly looking, with a gentle Kentucky accent; he'd been a Rhodes Scholar. In 1940, he'd been called "Very likely, the most expert living 'reader' of difficult verse." In his class, I struggled to understand his ideas, and felt enriched when I did.

Robert Penn Warren, also a Rhodes Scholar, was best known for his Pulitzer Prize–winning novel, *All the King's Men*, about 1930s Southern politics. He and Brooks produced two "New Criticism" books. He was good-looking and red-haired, and wore elegant, rumpled clothes. He read parts of a long verse narrative he was writing, which centered around a murder in the family of Thomas Jefferson's sister, to his students, and we became, in a way, his collaborators (after reading, he asked for comments). This was thrilling. A *New York Times* review called the result Warren's best book. In 1986, he was appointed America's first poet laureate.

One of the most popular undergraduate courses was Twentieth Century American Prose, taught by Norman Holmes Pearson, who had also studied in England and had coedited books with W. H. Auden and William Rose Benet. Pearson's back was deformed, and he walked with a limp—but starting in 1942, he served in London in the Offices of Strategic Services (the predecessor of the CIA), carrying out deception projects for the Normandy invasion; for this, he was decorated by three nations. He was briefly my faculty advisor, and visits to his office left me with a warm, tea-and-crumpets feeling. We'll return to him later.

Another popular course was Vincent Scully's world art history survey. Then a twenty-eight-year-old instructor, Scully became a full professor, and *Time* magazine twice called him one of the country's best college teachers. His main focus was on architecture and its relationship with the landscape; how it defines culture; and the architect's responsibility toward the community. He had great enthusiasm and vigorous opinions: Boston's City Hall, he once said, was "an uncouth monster, laying about itself with Neanderthalic roarings and tearing the very center of Boston to pieces." In Athens, in 1988, my wife, Patty, and I visited the Acropolis. A man was standing in front of the Parthenon, shouting at a group of American tourists. "Look at the crazy man," Patty said. I said, "That's Scully." One of the tourists told me, "He's been shouting at us all around Greece. It's wonderful!" In the mid-forties, Scully asked Frank Lloyd Wright to design a house for him. Concerning a rival American architect, Wright said, "Son, architecture began when I began building houses out there on the prairie." "What a confidence man," Scully said, "what a crook! He was great!" In the end, Scully did his own design. (Incidentally, Scully's students had assigned seats. During exams, the guy to my right often got his answers by peeking at *my* answers. He later became a Hollywood movie producer.)

* * *

By junior year, I'd discovered what Trollope called "the light that lies in a lady's eyes," and on weekends was hitch-hiking a great distance—to Cambridge, Massachusetts—on weekends to see Franny. She was two years older and worked as a teacher's assistant. She was pretty, with springy, curly brown hair. Her parents had a vacation house in New Hampshire. One Sunday, we trudged through heavy snow up the area's highest mountain (Monadnock), confident we'd be the only people at the summit, and found an English couple brewing tea. Franny and I were close for a time, but then I stopped hitchhiking. A year later, I got a "Dear John" letter:

Because I consider you a good friend, I thought I'd write to tell you some exciting news before it appears in the paper ... I am announcing my engagement on May third ... I am terribly happy about the whole thing ... Sometime I would love to have you meet him—I assume that you don't feel antagonistic because I am certainly not trying to say, "Ha, ha, *now* aren't you sorry?" As a parting thought, I don't regret any of last year ...

I spent the summer between junior and senior years in Europe, thanks to my agency earnings and a nine-hundred-dollar insurance company check (five years before, I'd suffered light damage in a car accident; today, a lawyer would get a hundred times that much). A Little Compton friend and I went over on the *Queen Elizabeth* in third class (when we weren't visiting first class, courtesy of a friendly steward). In a London pub, we were tipped off about Rushton Smutty, an entry that evening in one of the greyhound races at a stadium on the edge of town. We heard indecipherable Cockney accents and saw characters straight out of Dickens— and Rushton Smutty won handily, bringing us several pounds. In Paris, we found the hotel where Lloyd and Edith had stayed twenty-four years before; the rates were still reasonable, and the communal toilet was still in the hallway. On Bastille Day, we spent a thrilling evening in the crowd on the Champs Élysées: fireworks, parading troops, and—again and again, with crashing drums and shrieking trumpets—the world's most stirring anthem, the *Marseillaise*. I can't say I fell instantly in love with the city—it seemed confusing, and communicating wasn't easy—but I saw the beauty, and knew I wanted to come back.

An ad in the *Paris Herald Tribune* offered a World War II Jeep for two-hundred and fifty dollars. There were two hundred thousand miles on the odometer; it was painted robin's egg blue, and a decal on the windshield showed the Union Jack and proclaimed, "We drink tea, Britain's national drink" (this was the year of the Festival of Britain). We went to a government office to register the Jeep, but every official we approached said, "I'm starting my coffee break" and walked away. After an hour of this, a bystander whispered that he could arrange things for just a few francs; minutes later, we were out the door.

In our odd vehicle, often taken for Britishers because of the Union Jack, we headed south, lunching on bread and cheese and sleeping in dollar-a-night youth hostels. These were supposed to be for hikers and bicyclists only, but we were welcome because the Jeep was so primitive: you had to push it to start it, the canvas roof leaked, and it wouldn't go over forty-five miles per hour. We dutifully visited important cultural spots; I particularly liked the Lascaux cave paintings, the oldest paintings in the world. One day, we came upon the sweaty, hunched, swiftly pumping, bright-jerseyed, packed-together cyclists of the Tour de France, tearing through a tiny village as the entire population lined the street and cheered. We'd never heard of the Tour, but we were fascinated and decided to follow it for three days. In the main squares of the towns where the racers and their raffish but fiercely hardworking support teams spent the night, there was wine, accordion music, dancing, and fireworks. One of that year's most colorful stars was "Il Campionissimo," thirty-two-year-old, Italian-born Fausto Coppi, who'd won in '49 (and repeated in '52; he also won the Ciro d'Italia five times). An ex-butcher, Coppi had broken many bones while racing, and in his first victory, at age fifteen, had won twenty lira and a salami sandwich. Today, illegal drugs have soiled the Tour de France, but in '51 there were no rules against amphetamines ("la bomba"), and Coppi relied on them. Asked if most riders took them, he replied, "Yes, and those who claim otherwise, it's not worth talking to them about cycling." (Coppi didn't win the Tour we watched—the victor was a Swiss named Hugo Koblet.)

We turned east along the Riviera, then drove down to Florence, then Rome. Next came Venice, then north toward the Brenner Pass. Late one evening in the Dolomite Mountains—the slopes nearly killed the Jeep—the owner of a small roadside place told us that all she had left for dinner was coniglio.

She didn't speak English and we didn't speak Italian; before eating it, we wanted to know what coniglio was. With sign language and squeals, clucks, and bleats, we imitated a barnyard full of creatures, but always got, "No, that's not coniglio."

Then I twitched my nose, and indicated floppy ears, and asked, warping my meager French into "Italian," "Is it 'lapino'?"

She was horrified: "No, no, it's not 'lapino'!" She rushed outdoors, then, holding it by the ears, she plumped a fat, terrified, black and white rabbit onto the table and declared, "Coniglio, not 'lapino.'"

This mystified us totally, but we were hungry. The bunny stared at us wide-eyed; in sign language, we said, "Okay, coniglio, but we don't want to eat *him*." Plates of delicious, already-cooked rabbit stew soon arrived. We later learned that "coniglio" means domestic rabbit; my made-up word, "lapino," sounded sort of like "lepre," Italian for hare—and hare can be diseased.

Back in Paris, we were determined to recoup our two hundred and fifty dollars. *Herald Tribune* ads didn't work, so we drove the Jeep to a town where a new U.S. Air Force base had just opened, put a sign on the windshield, and sold it instantly. Later, sending the second of three payments, the buyer wrote that we'd escaped disaster: the Jeep "broke down completely" on the second day he owned it. "I'm still repairing it," he said, "but I'm glad to have it." Coming home on an overcrowded, low-cost student ship called the *Nellie* took ten days: triple-decker bunks crammed together, wretched food, wretched weather, and seasick scholars throwing up (memories of Yale Seabreeze parties). My friend and I had a bottle of gin for the cocktail hours, but he was sick all the way across, and I had to drink it all. He later served in the Navy aboard a submarine rescue ship and felt terrible half the time.

* * *

By senior year, as at Loomis, I'd become content with my studies and surroundings. I had friends. Especially in the spring, the campus was beautiful. I grinned when the band played *Boola, Boola*, or *March, March on down the Field*. I'd learned how to deal with abusive suit-pressing agency customers: when they started their condescension, I froze my face and stared silently into their eyes. (Woody Grumney, the coolheaded shortstop, was really good at that. Although I could handle those who basked in unearned privilege, I've disliked them ever since: their ilk produced the criminally stupid George W. Bush.) The air was often jumping with bells; I lived close to Harkness Tower, so I heard them clearly. Speaking of towers, I knew I was living in an ivory one, and I liked the feeling a lot—who wouldn't?

The military draft was still in force, and most of my classmates were going into the armed services after graduation, but I had a two-year deferment thanks to my long-ago emphysema, so I needed a job. Writing appealed to me greatly, but I couldn't support myself that way: thanks to my agency job, during the past four years I'd had no time to write, and had gained no experience. The closest I could come to writing would be editing; in a letter to the college-run employment office, I said that's what I wanted to do. On a whim, I added that I'd like something that involved foreign travel.

In April, a note appeared in my mailbox, asking me to go to New Haven's largest hotel, the Taft, at a certain hour. I found a crowd of classmates in the lobby; they said that Yale's ex-crew coach, Skip Walz, was in a room upstairs, giving fifteen-minute interviews. No one knew what company he was recruiting for.

In his early forties, Walz was big, good-looking, and hearty. He was sitting on one of the twin beds with a pile of folders beside him. He greeted me cordially, asked me a few general questions, then studied my folder and said, "I see you've had spontaneous mediastinal emphysema. Would that keep you from jumping out of an airplane wearing a parachute?"

"Probably not," I said, "but I'm not jumping out of an airplane."

Walz rose and shook my hand. "Thanks for coming."

At that time, almost no one had heard of the CIA. An authoritative book says that Walz was their chief recruiter, and "delivered 25 men ... to be trained for *parachutage* behind the Iron Curtain" (several were killed). The book also says that Yale had a long, close relationship with the CIA—which explains why Walz had been given my health records, which I'd naturally assumed were confidential. The book says that when Walz found likely candidates, he introduced them to higher-ups "who would apply the appropriate persuasion." One of those higher-ups was none other than my faculty advisor, genial, totally harmless-seeming Norman Holmes Pearson—he'd moved on from the OSS to the CIA. A classmate who met with Pearson told me that Pearson didn't try "appropriate persuasion;" on the contrary, "Pearson took me to Mory's for lunch and asked a lot of questions. He was testing how badly I wanted to join—how deep my interest was. At the end of lunch, he said, 'I don't think you really want to do this'—but I signed on anyway."

I never saw Skip Walz again, and I regret that, because he was colorful. He'd been a boxer and a sports announcer; as a naval lieutenant, he'd won a Bronze star in the Normandy invasion. During crew practice on the river, he yelled at the men pulling the oars, "Hook it, squeeze it, you're not digging clams with it! Come on, coxie, get away from that bank—you don't have wheels on that boat! Think! Think! Think!" At the time, I wasn't angry that Yale had given Walz my health records—those were Cold War days—but now I see how invasive and *wrong* it was.

One of the CIA's best-known operatives was Richard Bissell, who helped to plan the Bay of Pigs invasion. My good friend John Bissell, the fabric exporter and Indian school founder, was his nephew. A newspaper correspondent once asked John if it was a problem being associated with a famous spy and he replied that early in his life in India, his uncle asked if he would consider "doing anything." John was enraged by the question, and said it would ruin his life in India if it were known that his uncle had approached him.

* * *

As everyone knows, Yale has changed greatly since 1952. Today half the students are women—which must make the place infinitely more rewarding for men (Professor Peyre would certainly agree). In '52, if women were found in our rooms after a certain hour, there was hell to pay; in 2008, during student-run Sex Week, a visiting female professor stated—and nobody was shocked—"What I say to men when they think the vibrator will replace them is, 'This is not your competition, it's your colleague.'" Many years ago, Yale ceased to be an ivory tower. In the spring of 1970, when eight members of the Black Panthers were about to go on trial in New Haven for murder and kidnapping, university president Kingman Brewster created headlines by publicly stating that he doubted that the Panthers could get a fair trial anywhere in the U.S., and a majority of the students went on a two-week classroom strike, many of them saying they were protesting the Panthers' trial and pushing Yale to improve its relations with the black community. In my time, twenty years before, the most newsworthy protest was the four-hour-long Humpty Dumpty Riot (many injuries and arrests) which started when students got involved in an argument between a Good Humor ice cream truck driver and an independent ice cream seller whose truck was marked Humpty Dumpty (commendably, most of the students were on the side of Humpty, the underdog). I like to think that if the Yale administration, my classmates, and I had been faced with a challenge like the one in 1970, we would have responded with equal conscience and fervor—but of course we'll never know.

Seven

BESTSELLERLAND

Seated behind his antique desk in his grand office in Philadelphia, the chairman of the board of the Curtis Publishing Company—which put out the *Saturday Evening Post* and other magazines—steepled his fingers and studied me sympathetically as I tried to explain my hopes concerning a career in writing or editing.

An air raid siren started howling; in 1952, many U.S. cities staged practice alarms. The chairman flicked an intercom switch and asked, "What do I do?"

"Go into your private bathroom."

This facility was so deluxe that the toilet paper roll cried out to be called "un rouleau de papier hygiénique." The chairman leaned against the sink and asked, "What were you saying?"

That interview, arranged by a distant cousin of mine, was the first of several that led nowhere. I also saw a high-up editor of *Life* magazine (who wasn't pleased that I hadn't worked for any publications at Yale); genial, gentlemanly Tim Coward, the head of his own small book publishing firm; and an editor at another publishing house who lived up to expectations by drinking three martinis at lunch. Then I heard about the training program at Doubleday & Company.

Doubleday was then one of the giants of book publishing. Its bestselling authors included Edna Ferber, Herman Wouk, Thomas Costain, Leon Uris, Irving

Stone, and Daphne du Maurier. Its backlist—Somerset Maugham, Rudyard Kipling, Bram Stoker, Upton Sinclair, Aldous Huxley, T. E. Lawrence, and others—was a gold mine. The company printed its books at presses it owned in Garden City, New York, and in Pennsylvania, Maryland, and Virginia. To sell those books—and those of other publishers—it owned a chain of thirty bookstores in twenty-five cities, and many highly successful book clubs, including the Literary Guild. The company was founded in 1897 by Frank Nelson Doubleday and a partner. Among its first bestsellers was *A Day's Work* by Kipling who, using Doubleday's initials, gave him his lasting nickname, "Effendi," which means "chief" in Turkish. The company's ownership has changed several times; it is now a division of Random House.

This enormous operation was, of course, designed to make money. Some trainees had the highfalutin' notion that book publishing was all about *literature*; to teach us that it was a *business*, and that satisfying customer demand was vital, we spent our first two months as sales clerks in Doubleday stores. The store where I labored in the fall of '52 was on the ground floor of Lord & Taylor, the luxury department store that catered mostly to women. I soon realized that most customers weren't buying books for their own pleasure, or to increase their knowledge; they were buying them as gifts, mainly for people in the hospital (this was when patients *read*, instead of staring at TV). As Christmas approached, sales rose; those volumes would wind up under the tree.

The roughest parts of the job were being on my feet all day and coping with the hostility of the store manager, a hatchet-faced harridan with unwashed hair who'd decided that I was somehow part of management, and had been sent to spy on her. As at all book publishing companies in those days, the pay for beginners was abysmal: at the suit-pressing agency, I'd made twenty-five dollars a week; now I was getting thirty-five dollars. We did get a small commission on each sale and a double commission on books published by Doubleday. One of those, *The Caine Mutiny*, had recently come out, so when a customer asked for a recommendation, the answer was easy. One day, I was approached by a shy, early middle-aged couple. Their daughter, they whispered, was reaching the age when she should learn "the facts of life"; would *The Kinsey Report* do the job? Shame on me, I sold it to them. My fellow clerks were congenial, especially dark-haired, dark-eyed Esther, who'd just graduated from Smith. Because she knew exactly how little I was earning, I could take her to inexpensive restaurants in the evening without blushing; afterwards, we'd go to her apartment and of course talk about how many copies of *The Caine Mutiny* we'd sold that day.

From the start, I told the head of the training program—a forceful, bustling woman who was also the head of the publicity department and the wife of *Time* magazine's most important book reviewer—that I wanted to wind up in the editorial department. Shortly after Christmas, I reported for duty in a humble office squeezed among larger, handsomer ones. My job— reading the "slush pile" of unsolicited manuscripts— was "the velvet hammer treatment": each boring, badly written submission was a small tap between the eyes, and by day's end, you had a serious headache. My orders were, "If a submission looks hopeless, read only enough to confirm that, then send it back with our standard rejection letter; if it shows any promise *whatsoever*, pass it along to a junior editor."

All of my "passalongs" were ultimately rejected— except for *Buckskin and Blanket Days*, an account of American Indian life in the late 1800s written by a gun-toting newspaperman/circuit preacher who married an

Indian woman and ran for the U.S. vice presidency on the Populist ticket. It was exciting reading; Doubleday's print ads called it "A MAJOR LITERARY FIND!" and the *Saturday Evening Post* ran three long excerpts from it. It earned Doubleday many dollars and me some pats on the back—but no increase in pay.

After a couple of months of the slush pile, another trainee took over, and I was given more interesting tasks. I commented on manuscripts that had been bought but had problems, suggesting cuts, pointing out where the writing could be clearer, and so on. The company was thinking of starting a line of books on fishing; I looked into the commercial possibilities and after taking several authors of books and articles about fishing—and an agent with the wonderful name Lurton Blassingame—out to lunch (my first, giddy expense account experience), I wrote a report saying that the field was too specialized for Doubleday. I completely rewrote *How to Buy a Used Car*. The author, a nice guy who earned his living in a crooked business, was a rotten writer, but had useful tips: "If the car smells of bananas, beware: they're been stuffed into the transmission to deaden the noise of clashing gears."

Gradually, I got to know editors, sales reps, art department members, and others. Just like Lloyd when he was at Macmillan, I had to deal with crazies who got off the elevator carrying manuscripts and wouldn't leave without making a pitch.

Doubleday occupied three floors of 575 Madison Avenue; the editorial floor's reception room was posh—thick carpeting, soft lighting, and Doubleday books discreetly displayed. Behind a mahogany desk was the classiest receptionist in all of New York, middle-aged Mrs. DeBanzie, a gently reared English lady with an upper crust accent, tasteful clothes, and a jolly laugh. My phone would ring, and she'd say, "There's someone who'd like to make a presentation." Donning the jacket of my gray flannel suit, I'd wonder what I'd encounter this time. Another reincarnated Jesus? Another inventor of a perpetual motion machine? If the visitor insisted on talking for more than five minutes, Mrs. DeBanzie would somehow cause her phone to ring, answer it, and softly say, "Mr. Goodrich, you're wanted in your office." It worked every time.

Copy editing—"comma-chasing"—was demanding and dreary. At Doubleday, a mild-mannered man in his thirties did the job in a small office, surrounded by encyclopedias and foreign language dictionaries. His expression told you he wasn't happy—but then, unexpectedly, he got a hefty inheritance; it took him only half an hour to clean out his desk. Another boring job was writing sales promotion copy; the bright, funny man who did it brought the wrong guy home from a gay bar one night and was murdered.

I've always felt that the secretaries at book publishing companies are a cut above the average in brains, looks—you name it. Kay Ullman was my age, a Vassar graduate, and pretty, with springy curls that accounted for her nickname, Fuzzy. We often had lunch together. She wanted a more challenging job and a husband, and she got both; his last name was Brush, so she became Fuzzy Brush. Her new job was assistant to a leading literary agent—and in future years, she helped me greatly.

The company president, Douglas Black, was stout and white-haired and always looked worried. A couple of times, when I passed his office, he invited me in and asked in a fatherly way if I liked my work. Those invitations were well-meant—but I always felt that he was checking me out: in hiring Goodrich, had Doubleday blundered? Black had worked his way through Columbia Law School as a night clerk in a Doubleday bookstore, then had become the company's lawyer, then its president (in 1946). He was a friend of President Eisenhower, and Doubleday published Eisenhower's books (and President Truman's and General McArthur's, and on and on). There was a pro-Eisenhower bent at Doubleday: during the first race between him and Adlai Stevenson, I was chided for wearing a Stevenson lapel button (showing a shoe sole with a hole in it). Douglas Black had an unmarried daughter my age. He once asked me to join a weekend party at his vacation house. I'd planned to go to Sakonnet for the weekend, so I declined. A female fellow-employee was shocked: "You've hurt your chances here!"

Because I wanted to be one of them, the people in the company who interested me most were the editors. There were maybe a dozen of them, mostly men—except for the cookbook and (interestingly) crime book editors. The floor that housed the editorial offices was hushed and formal: carpeted corridors, secretaries (some elderly) behind desks, editors behind closed doors. Once a week, the editors and people from the sales, art, sales promotion, and subsidiary rights departments met in the conference room to discuss suggestions for new books and payments to be made. Notes on these meetings were distributed around the company and all carried the same label, "All terms mentioned in this meeting are for the purpose of discussion only and are not final. In any case, they are absolutely confidential." I'm sure that that confidentiality was almost never breached: book publishing was then a business for ladies and gentlemen. The notes on one meeting praised my report on fishing books—but that didn't get me a raise either.

The weekly meetings were warm and congenial, with much laughter (why not? The company was plenty prosperous) and also intensely serious: sometimes, big money was at stake. The business-suited higher-ups sat around a large, rectangular table with papers and water glasses before them; their assistants, including me, sat behind them. I felt honored to be there, and doubly honored on the (rare) occasions when I was asked to comment. Once, there were questions about the proposed dust jacket for an Edna Ferber novel: was the one-word title shown boldly enough to be clearly visible in a bookstore? The art director excused herself, taking the actual-sized sketch with her. Minutes later, we meeting members looked out the window: across the full width of Madison Avenue, the art director stood in the window of a friend's office, and we easily read the title, *GIANT*. The people at those meetings cared about profits, but, unlike some in publishing today, they were in no way crass. If someone had suggested, "Let's publish O. J. Simpson's 'confession,'" everyone else would have silently left the room.

Tim Seldes was the youngest editor I took my "passalongs" to. I'd known him at Dalton: he was taller and a few years older, and had the good luck to be Marian Seldes' brother (their father was the well-known critic and author, Gilbert Seldes). I recall Tim as a quipster: "Good morrow, young fellah!" He later left Doubleday and took over one of New York's best literary agencies.

Also young and tall was Sam Vaughan, who later became Editor in Chief. Sam was funny; I recall his story about shopping for a new mattress: a salesman said that resistance to "body ash" was important. Sam edited the work of some fine writers, including William F. Buckley Jr., who regularly thanked him on the Acknowledgments pages of his books:

> Every time Sam devotes himself to a manuscript I give him, I come out of the experience with the sense of a book reinvented, so extraordinary are his contributions

and

> I was asked by Samuel Vaughan ... please
> not to mention yet again his extraordinary
> editorial ability, kindness, generosity, and
> care, so I won't.

Yet another young editor was Clarkson N. Potter: horn-rimmed glasses, slicked-back blond hair. After lunch one day, he and I went to a French-language bookstore in Rockefeller Center and picked up a smuggled copy of Vladimir Nabokov's *Lolita*. It had been published in Paris by a "dirty books" press, then banned in France and England; Nabokov was trying to find an American publisher. Clark told me that our pickup broke U.S. law. In the end, Doubleday passed—which they regretted, because the book was an enormous critical and financial success. Clark later left Doubleday and started his own company, naming it after himself and specializing in coffee table books. Suffering poor health, he had to sell the company; after recovering, he started a new one, but to his great annoyance couldn't put his own name on its books—without realizing it, he'd *sold* his name. "There are 'Clarkson N. Potter' books on the market," he told me, "that *this* Clarkson N. Potter never heard of!"

Doubleday's many successful cook, travel, decorating, and bird books were edited by Clara Claasen. She started at the company in 1929, and when I met her was a blondish, well-dressed lady well able to hold her own against her male colleagues. She also edited nine bestselling historical novels by Pulitzer Prize winner Kenneth Roberts (*Northwest Passage, Arundel, Rabble in Arms*, among others). In addition to being strong-minded, she must have been something of a saint: a *New York Times* article once called Roberts "truculent, irascible, cantankerous, arrogant, sardonic, blunt, prickly, blustering, exuberant," and "a man perpetually at war with life and the world."

Many plausible-sounding proposals crossed the desk of Doubleday's Managing Editor, Walter Bradbury. At a typical 1953 meeting, he asked for comments on a possible biography of Sir James Barry; a German mountain-climbing team's report on their efforts in the Himalayas; and a history of the U.S. flag. All were turned down, even though the Society of Mayflower Descendants had said they'd buy five thousand copies of the flag book. "Brad" was the man who had me look into books about fishing—another turndown. We got along especially well; years later, when I was freelancing, he gave me an excellent book idea, which I stupidly ignored. He was the firm's science-fiction editor, and worked closely with Isaac Asimov and Ray Bradbury (no kin).

Executive Editor LeBaron Russell Barker Jr., second from the top, handled a heavy load of twenty-five or thirty books a year. His authors included Irving Stone, Herman Wouk, Robert Graves, Robert Ruark, and Arthur Hailey, who said he had "an uncanny instinct for what would work and would not work in fiction." Born in Plymouth, Massachusetts, he came across as a New England patrician; to me, he seemed distant and intimidating. He asked me to comment on a few manuscripts, and I was proud when he said that some of his authors said I'd helped them.

The man leading these talented individuals was Editor in Chief Kenneth D. McCormick. Many people thought he was the best in the business; he was once called "a teacher of two generations of editors and tireless defender of the right to read ... No other editor/publisher ... has been responsible for so many good, successful, and lasting books; no one has brought so much reading pleasure to so large and varied an audience."

Ken's career was a classic American story. His father was a minister; he grew up in Oregon and went to Willamette University, then travelled around Europe and the Middle East, then hitchhiked across the country to New York, where he became a clerk in several Doubleday bookstores. His first editorial job was slush-pile-reading; he said it gave him ulcers, exhaustion, and a promotion to assistant editor. He then rose to full editor; in 1942, on the recommendation of Somerset Maugham, he got the top job. He was good-looking and plainspoken, with a kind of Jimmy Stewart Americanness. He worked standing at a desk attached to the wall, and was always welcoming when I interrupted him with a question. Having myself clerked and been slush-smothered, I felt a kinship—which he seemed to return: he was an open, generous man. The week he retired, the top three—*one, two, and three*—novels on *The New York Times* Bestseller List had been edited by him. Asked once how he felt about a review of one of his bestsellers that said the author couldn't write, he replied (no doubt with one of his warm grins), "They should've seen the manuscript before I worked on it."

* * *

Because of its many bestsellers, Doubleday was sometimes called too commercial. True, it won the bestseller game—but that wasn't the whole story. In 1953, its youngest editor, twenty-five-year-old Jason Epstein, created Anchor Books, the first American line of truly distinguished paperbacks. Their specialty was reprinting prestigious, neglected works of fiction and nonfiction at low prices; the series has been growing (and making money) ever since. Jason was married to equally young, equally brilliant Barbara Zimmerman, who edited some of Doubleday's better authors. In 1951, Doubleday bought the U.S. rights to *The Diary of Anne Frank*, and Barbara was chosen as editor. She was the same age Anne would have been if she'd lived, and soon grew close to Anne's father, Otto, who suggested that they ask Eleanor Roosevelt to write the introduction.

When the book was published, several people suspected that Barbara had actually written the very moving piece, and Mrs. Roosevelt had signed it. As of 2006, *The Diary* had been translated into sixty-seven languages, and over thirty-million copies had been sold. In 1963, when a one-hundred-and-fourteen-day strike shut down all New York newspapers—which meant no book reviews or advertising—Barbara, Jason, and two writer friends started the *New York Review of Books*, which over the next decades became (*Esquire* magazine said) "the premier literary-intellectual magazine in the English language." With a coeditor, Barbara ran the *Review* until her death in 2006. At Doubleday, I briefly worked in a corner of her office. She'd been born with only one hand, and it was amazing to see how efficiently she coped—typing, juggling the phone while taking notes ...

(Many of the first Anchor covers were drawn by tall, bearded, oddly costumed—high-top sneakers and a raccoon coat—Edward Gorey. Gorey began publishing his own strange books in '53. The drawings were intricate and meticulous; the stories were mysterious and morbid. In *The Willowdale Handcar*, two men and a woman pumped their way through Bogus Corners and Gristleburg, and admired a collection of seven thousand glass telephone pole insulators. In *The Gashlycrumb Tinies*, children from A to Z met grotesque ends: "A is for Amy, who fell down the stairs, B is for Basil, assaulted by bears." In his Doubleday office, Gorey had a grisly bronze "memento mori": a six-inch-long skeleton being gnawed by tiny rats.)

* * *

During this time, I spent off-duty hours trying to write short stories. By now, I'd begun to find real pleasure in writing. Not in first drafts—they're the toughest, and after an hour my shirt would be damp in the armpits—but in rewriting: cutting, adding, reshaping.

Writing, I realized, *is* rewriting: while you're doing it, you find out what you really want to say. I sent one of my stories to the mother of a Dalton friend, Nick Wood, the bathtub-blaster; she was an assistant fiction editor at *The New Yorker*. Her rejection letter said she felt I had talent—but writing was a complicated craft that couldn't be learned quickly; I shouldn't expect to be published right away. That, of course, was sound advice—but I recall feeling, with youthful hubris, "Why shouldn't I get to the top now?"

(Mrs. Wood was close to *The New Yorker*'s famous couple, E. B. and Katherine White. One New Year's Eve, while Nick and I were still in college, he and I had drinks in Times Square, then more drinks at the Whites' Turtle Bay house, where I passed out in a bathroom. I was awakened by Mr. White shouting, "Unlock the door!" Lying on the floor, I mumbled that I couldn't see the lock, because the bathroom light was off. "Then *turn on* the light!" It was sort of like a *New Yorker* story by James Thurber. Nick helped me into a taxi. In future years, the Whites spent more time in their vacation house in Brooklin, Maine; perhaps my visit influenced them ...)

* * *

On the East Eighties streets of Yorkville, people spoke German, and shops offered food from the Fatherland. In the early 1930s, my nursemaid, Pearl, used to push my stroller to East 86th Street, where large men in jackboots and uniforms bearing a curious emblem paraded with a brass band. I thought these goose-stepping fellows were wonderful. When they heard about these expeditions, my parents yelled, "That's the German-American Bund! They're Nazis!" No more brass bands.

Now, while working at Doubleday, I went to Yorkville for luscious wurst and to visit a noisy beer hall where the proprietor wore lederhosen, played the accordion, and sang, drunkenly, "How much iss zat doggie in ze vindow, / Ze von mit der voggily schvantz?" Most evenings, my date was gentle, smiling Joan. I also took forgetful Mary Kaplan. One night, outside her parents' empty, Upper East Side townhouse, she realized she didn't have keys. "Reach up to that balcony," she said. "The window there's unlocked. Then take the elevator down and let me in." While I was clinging to the ironwork like Cary Grant in *To Catch a Thief*, a police car's searchlight hit me. It took Mary many words to save me from arrest.

(Mary's father, Jacob M. Kaplan, made millions by selling molasses and owning Welch's Grape Juice. In 1971, his nephew, imprisoned in Mexico on a murder charge—many believed he'd been framed—stepped on board a helicopter that landed in the prison yard. Jacob Kaplan said he knew nothing about the escape—which was made into a movie starring Charles Bronson. Years later, having ghosted another famous man's autobiography, I suggested to Mr. Kaplan that if he wanted to publish his own life story, I could help—but he'd have to tell the truth about the Mexican jailbreak. He smiled.)

Another of my evening companions was Edmund Duffy's bright, funny daughter, Sara. I met her at her parents' East Sixties brownstone, where I also met *The New Yorker* writers John McNulty and Geoffrey Hellman. McNulty seemed the embodiment of the characters in his short Third Avenue barroom pieces—compactly built, sardonic, unmistakably Irish—and was often sloshed. He and Mr. Duffy went to the races a lot. I kept suggesting to Mr. Duffy that he write a book about his life and friends; sadly, he never did. One summer weekend, I visited the Duffys' house on Cape Cod.

Walking along a narrow path through the dunes, Sara
and I suddenly came upon a thin, beautiful, fey woman
wearing history's tiniest bikini. "Daphne Hellman," Sara
said. "Geoffrey's ex-wife. She plays jazz on the harp."
That sounded odd, but I heard her later, and she was
wonderful. She and Hellman—who seemed stolid and
owlish—didn't get along; I heard that once, after an
argument, they were in a crowded, silent elevator, and
she reached behind herself and gave his testicles a hard
squeeze. Sara liked their teenage son; in a Broadway
movie palace, the three of us, wearing nose-pinching,
cardboard-framed spectacles, stared at a pioneering 3-
D flick. I wrote a short story about my trip to Cape
Cod; the title, *For Her Sweet Face and My New Clothes*,
was a line from a poem by Scott Fitzgerald. The story
was rejected by *The New Yorker* (and other magazines).
I still hadn't made a sale, but I persisted.

Sara and I remained friends. A few years later, she
married Ivan Chermayeff, who succeeded mightily as a
designer of corporate logos (NBC, Mobil, PBS, and
others). As an engagement present, Ivan gave Sara a
collage he'd made from torn-up blue jeans. Sara loved
it, and hung it, framed, over the living room fireplace.
When Mr. Duffy, a traditionalist, saw it, he wasn't
pleased (he'd already privately dubbed his son-in-law-
to-be "Ivan the Terrible Artist"). Duffy was the last to
go to bed; the next morning, Sara found the collage
hanging upside down. She righted it and said nothing.
The next night, the same thing happened. Sara's mother
finally got Duffy to quit. Duffy and Ivan must ultimately
have become friends: it was Ivan who organized a
memorial party for Duffy after Duffy died.

On summer weekends and vacations, I went to
Sakonnet. Now legally an adult, I could go in the
evenings to the big, ramshackle, shingled, one-story
Fo'c's'le, which perched perilously on barnacled stilts
at the water's edge, overlooking the harbor. The dining

room smelled of boiled lobster and dense, doughy clam fritters ("Drop one on your foot, and you'll break your toes"). The barroom had a U-shaped bar with stools bolted to the floor so drunks couldn't tip them over and smelled of Narragansett beer and Lucky Strike cigarettes. By 9:00, the chatter and laughter flooded out into the parking lot. The patrons were town and gown—summer people and "natives"; they got along fine. I knew that whenever I dropped in, I'd find friends. I've never felt so at home in a place that wasn't home. The owner used to put his Boston bull terrier on the bar, with a newspaper under him "for cleanliness," and tell colorful stories about his days as a rumrunner.

Among the barroom regulars was my cousin Cang Lloyd. He'd come in midmorning, give the bartender a ten-dollar bill, and get back twenty half-dollars. Drinks cost fifty cents; by day's end, Cang's pockets were empty. Another regular was Louie, a burly fisherman with a jutting jaw and a reddish crewcut. If I ran into Louie away from The Fo'c's'le and asked how he was, he'd reply, "Sober, dammit, but we'll soon fix that." Then there was "Heinie" (real name, Henry), the bachelor scion of a leading Providence family. I believe he worked as a stockbroker. During the war, he'd served in the Navy as a high-ranking officer in charge of the port of Boston. One of his stories concerned the visit of a Russian warship whose officers were mostly women: "I took the ladies out on the town and tried to match them vodka for vodka. A disaster."

Heinie's cottage had a minute living-dining room. He used to invite me and others there after The Fo'c's'le closed, pull a rubber raft out of a closet, and, while sipping his nightcap, pump it full of air. As the thing grew, Heinie's guests were gradually pressed against the walls; eventually, some of us climbed into the raft. Heinie sometimes went fishing for striped bass in the raft. He sat at one end, pole in hand, and a friend sat at the other end. When swells passed under the raft, first one end rose, then the other, and it looked as though the two men were enjoying some strange, aquatic, amusement park ride. Over the years, Heinie lived with a series of good-natured "fiancées," each blonder than the last.

Edith had an elderly gardener, Peter, who was married to a younger woman. She got pregnant and he said, "I dunno who's de fada. I'm away all day. God knows what womens'll do." When his ancient truck broke down, he announced, "The fuckin' fucker's fucked."

The *Providence Journal* had a Society section, which ran every Sunday and covered the goings-on in Newport and other Rhode Island resort towns—Narragansett, Watch Hill, even little Little Compton. One August weekday, at the beach club, a reporter-photographer asked a cousin of mine, Matthew Finn, if he could take his picture. "Certainly," Matthew replied. "And your name?" In a thick French accent, rolling the R, Matthew said, "Francois DeTergent. Capital D, capital T." Matthew almost got away with it—but as the presses were about to start, a *Journal* editor said, "We'd better check this."

* * *

For several years, my soft-spoken, gentlemanly friend, Pyke Johnson, who encouraged me in my writing, was Doubleday's publicity director. When Jason Epstein left the company, Pyke became head of Anchor Books. In 1964, Doubleday had a sales department junior executive named Richard O'Connor take a business school course in marketing, exposing him to the world of product development, marketing plans, and market share. Back at Doubleday, at one of the weekly meetings, he called one of Pyke's Anchor Books a "product." O'Connor wrote that there was a momentary silence in the room full of editors and sales people. All eyes were on Pyke, whose face grew redder and redder. He turned toward O'Connor and slowly said, his voice rising with each word, "Young man, a book is not a PRODUCT!" O'Connor said that the last word came out like a snakebite. "What I could not appreciate," he continued, "was that I was witness to a changing of the guard from editorial control of publishing to power vested in marketing. For better or worse, publishing was in a sea change, which has not ended to this day." Two years later, O'Connor was named Doubleday's first-ever marketing director.

Thank God, while I was at Doubleday, that sea change (which soon became a tsunami) hadn't yet started—but I had a change of my own to worry about. My two-year draft deferment had run out, I'd passed my Army physical exam, and I'd been ordered to report to a building in lower Manhattan on March 18, '54. I continued working through the seventeenth—I knew that two years were about to be painfully ripped out of my pleasant, interesting life, and I wanted to hang onto my routine as long as I could. My bosses promised that my job would be waiting when I got back—the Army was just a hiatus.

Tim Seldes and I used to have lunch every three weeks or so. About ten days before I was scheduled to leave, he asked if I'd like to have lunch again two days later. I said, "Sure." As we walked along East Fifty-Seventh Street toward the low-priced eateries on Third Avenue, he suddenly seized my arm and steered me toward an expensive French restaurant. I protested—"I can't afford this!"—but Tim growled something like, "Please shut up." At a table for five were two female editorial assistants I often worked with and Walter Bradbury. This lunch; Brad said, was the editorial department's send-off; Ken McCormick had helped him to plan it, but at the last minute couldn't come. The food and wine were splendid—and then Brad pulled a gift-wrapped package from under the table. Inside was a nifty, compact, European-made portable typewriter. "It's from the whole department," he said. "We took up a collection. Take it with you and write more stories." That lunch was one of the greatest things that ever happened to me.

Eight

RUMORS, BULLSHIT, AND LIES

On a sunny morning in late May 1954, wearing the uniform of a private in the U.S. Army and a stubbly G.I. haircut, in the best physical shape I'd been in in years thanks to two months of Basic Training at Fort Dix, in New Jersey, I sat beside the also-uniformed driver of a Jeep. He'd picked me and my barracks bag up at the railroad station in Fayetteville, North Carolina, and was delivering us to Smoke Bomb Hill, in Fort Bragg. The hill was home to the Special Warfare Center, where (the mimeographed orders in my pocket said) I would join Headquarters Company of the First Radio Broadcasting and Leaflet Battalion (I would come to call it "the First RB&L"—hence "rumors, bullshit, and lies"). On either side of the two-lane road was a vast pine forest; judging from the smoke, large parts of it were on fire. Overhead, a mile or two from the road, big, prop-driven planes lumbered through the air, and man-sized objects fell out of them, and white flowers burst open.

"What're those?" I asked, "And why are the woods burning?"

"Those fuckers are fuckin' paratroopers," the driver replied, "an' the fuckin' woods are fuckin' burnin' cause they're a fuckin' artillery range. You fuckin' sound like a fuckin' leg."

A leg (short for "straight-leg," meaning non-paratrooper) I was, and for the next two years I was looked down upon by the thousands of 'troopers stationed at Bragg, "The Home of the Airborne"; most of them talked like that driver. We psychological warfare (or Psywar) practitioners were considered eggheads, the lowest of the low, and we were given nasty jobs—like ash and trash (garbage collection) and prisoner chasing (guarding stockade inmates)—more often than other outfits on the post because our commanding officers were lightweights who couldn't shield us against those chores (serious, West Point–type officers shunned Psywar as a bad career move). One of the battalion commanders was a pleasant, mild-mannered Reservist—a civilian in uniform. Another was a sadist—he made you stand at rigid attention while you were speaking with him. He often proclaimed that he'd started his Army career thanks to dogs. "I was a night watchman at Macy's department store during World War II," he'd say, "which made me draft-exempt. Then they brought in German shepherds to guard the place and the Army got me."

Again, my luck was good: the Korean War had ended and the one in Vietnam hadn't started, so I wasn't going to be shot at. However, in this peacetime Army, morale was at rock bottom. Those of us who'd been drafted—and in the lower ranks we greatly outnumbered the career soldiers—had no sense of doing anything important; we were just marking time. Every draftee knew exactly how many days remained before his discharge; you'd sit down beside a guy in the mess hall and introduce yourself by saying, "I'm two hundred and twelve," and he'd respond with *his* number. In many ways, it was like prison.

The First Radio Broadcasting and Leaflet Battalion was housed in decrepit, wooden, two-story, World War II barracks on sandy soil, amidst countless pine trees. The buildings were chilly in winter and fiercely hot in summer—no air conditioning. Your iron, thin-mattressed bunk had to line up exactly with those on either side; so did your wall locker and foot locker. In the latrine, everyone pissed side by side into a trough; there was a row of toilet bowls without walls, doors, or drop-down seats. Sitting on a bowl, trousers around your ankles, you greeted friend and foe.

A key to military discipline has always been, dehumanize the lower ranks—make them defecate while others watch, bully them, run them ragged; it makes them docile. When I served, many senior sergeants, who are the true managers of the Army's day-to-day business, were Korean and World War II veterans, and they were convinced that soldiering (pronounced "sojerin'") should be rigorous, and draftees should keep their fuckin' mouths shut and obey even the most senseless orders—*or else*. In the First RB&L, senseless orders were commonplace. Once, before a colonel from the Office of the Inspector General arrived to check barracks cleanliness, we had to unscrew every lightbulb, wash it, and screw it back in. One of our officers, a recent graduate of a third-rate Southern agricultural college, was so anxious about this inspection that he ordered us to mop and scrub every inch of the latrine three times, then brought his madly blushing young wife in to check the results ("She's a real good housekeeper"). We were constantly ordered to pick up the pine cones that kept falling—who would have guessed it?—off the trees: "It makes the barracks area (pronounced "*ay*-rea") look better." We also made the *ay*-rea look better by whitewashing the trunks of the trees. As a teenager, I hadn't minded calling my teachers and other male elders "Sir"—they deserved respect. Now,

I had to call my inferiors "Sir," and it rankled. I also had to salute them. I did so religiously—only to ensure that they couldn't reprimand me from their loftiness.

A lot of that will sound familiar to men who were drafted then—but what made the situation truly galling, and laughable, was that unending chickenshit was loaded onto above-average, often highly educated inductees. ("Chickenshit," a word heard hundreds of times daily, can be defined as "menial tasks which keep the enlisted men busy while the upper ranks hang out in the officers' club.") Theoretically, the battalion's mission was to produce propaganda in several languages. Its equipment included Jeeps bearing loudspeakers, vans housing radio transmitters, and mobile presses capable of churning out tons of leaflets (when leaflets were dropped from Army aircraft in Korea, the enemy welcomed them as toilet paper). I'd been designated a "scriptwriter," and supplied with a typewriter and reams of paper, which I seldom got to use. Among the other draftees whose time was being wasted were:

Dark-haired, brooding, heavily accented Richard Mayer wound up in the First RB&L because he spoke— as I recall—Romanian. In civilian life, he'd been a stamp dealer; his footlocker contained hundreds of stamps, and he spent his evenings mailing them to customers and sending checks to his New York bank.

I became friends with Christopher Bird, one of our Russian-speakers. He was a Harvard-educated eccentric who later wrote a popular book titled *The Secret Life of Plants*. In it, Chris told the story of a scientist who, believing that his beloved houseplants could respond to his emotional changes, hooked the plants up to an electrical device that could record signals on paper, then went to bed with his girlfriend. Sure enough, the machine drew mountainous peaks at precisely the scientist's most ecstatic moments.

Another friend, Thomas Riha, was an Eastern European expert. Lightly built, fair-haired, and always smiling, he was born in Prague and came to the U.S. in 1947. He had a master's degree in modern Russian history; at Ft. Bragg, his job was shoveling coal into furnaces and water heaters. He urged me to get the same assignment: "It's easy, and furnace stokers never have to pick up pine cones or do guard duty or K. P. or any of that." I still have a CERTIFICATE OF PROFICIENCY saying that I was "deemed qualified to perform the duties of FIREMAN, FURNACES, AND WATER HEATERS," but I never actually stoked anything. Instead, I did plenty of the other stuff. K.P. was the toughest physical work I've ever lived through; it was the Augean stable plus Sisyphus' rock, with Sergeant Maldonado forever screaming at me.

(After the Army, Tom Riha got a PhD at Harvard. He came through New York occasionally, and we had lunch at a Czech restaurant featuring fruit soup. He wound up as an Associate Professor at the University of Colorado in Boulder. One day in March 1969, Tom didn't show up for classes. He wasn't at home. He was always fastidious, but his desk was littered with papers; he'd been doing his income taxes. The police started a search. Mrs. Galya Tannenbaum, a Denver friend of Tom's who'd once served two years in prison for forgery and embezzlement, claimed that Tom had told her he wouldn't be returning to Boulder and had asked her to settle his affairs. She forged his signature to sell his car and house and was charged with a felony. Court psychiatrists found her insane and sent her to the state mental hospital. Meantime, the authorities were investigating the demise of two other friends of Galya's—a man and a woman—who died of apparent cyanide poisoning before Tom's disappearance. In March '71, Galya killed herself in the hospital—with cyanide. People in Boulder are convinced she murdered Tom and dropped his body down one of the area's many abandoned mine shafts.)

Mate Meštrovic, another good friend, was our Serbo-Croat expert and the son of Yugoslavia's most-famous-ever artist, the sculptor Ivan Meštrovic. Mate later wrote for *Time* magazine, became a professor of European history at Fairleigh Dickinson University, and is currently the Croatian Ambassador to Bucharest— where, he says, everyone drives a Mercedes stolen in another country.

When I was assigned to Psychological Warfare, my first reaction was, "Interesting work!" Borden Stevenson told me he felt the same way. Borden was the second son of the great Adlai Stevenson. He was smart, good-looking, and a hit with women. He'd been to Choate and Harvard and knew many glitterati, including Italian noblemen, Lady Astor, and the future Aga Kahn. Despite his connections, he got no special treatment when dirty jobs were handed out, because the recent Army-McCarthy hearings had cast a dark light on favoritism. Borden and I became close; later, I'll describe some odd experiences we shared.

Another product of a famous family was Gilbert M. Grosvenor, heir to the cash-cow National Geographic Society. Gil later ran that organization and its magazine successfully, and was rewarded with thirteen honorary degrees and seats on the boards of corporations and charitable and preservation groups. At Ft. Bragg, during roll call, sergeants pronounced his name "Gros-nover."

Yorick Blumenfeld's father, Erwin, was one of the great fashion photographers of the thirties, forties, and fifties. Yorick had a germ phobia, and wore rubber gloves (which he bought himself) while on K. P. In the latrine, he put his booted feet on the toilet bowl's rim and squatted.

Our barracks were aggravatingly noisy, thanks in part to short, curly haired Ahmed, the battalion's only

Arabic-speaker: wearing a nightgown-like djibbah, he endlessly thumped a basketball on the linoleum floor. Incidentally, that floor caused no end of agony. For the frequent barracks inspections, it had to gleam like glass, so we spent many hours applying wax and pushing a crude electric buffer.

Because of the battalion's mission, and the foreign-born draftees in it, we always suspected there were CIA agents among us. Bayard Stockton, a reddish-haired, beefy, genial fellow, had gone to Williams College. After chatting with him, you came away thinking, *Something's going on there.* He got more weekend passes than the rest of us, and went to Washington "to see friends." An Internet piece says he was, in fact, in the CIA from '51 to '57—which covers his Army years. He then became a roving journalist and radio commentator. He wrote several books on the CIA, and lived in or visited sixteen different countries. In 1959, I visited his office in London, where he was *Newsweek*'s bureau chief. Sitting there with sleeves rolled up, cigarette smouldering, hammering his typewriter, he looked jaded and packed with intrigue. He finally settled in California. According to the online article, "years after he left the CIA, his house was burgled by people trying to find papers he might have retained. After his death, his family found countless guns stashed throughout the house."

For many weeks in 1968, Adam Smith's *The Money Game* was number one on *The New York Times* Bestseller List. In 1971, Smith's *Supermoney* was also number one. From 1984 to 1997, one of the most respected shows on PBS TV was *Adam Smith's Money World*. Adam Smith's real name is George Jerome Waldo Goodman, and when he and I first met, he'd already accomplished a lot: Harvard cum laude, Rhodes Scholar, and author of a well-regarded "coming of age" novel. He was brown-haired, medium-sized, wore horn-rimmed glasses, and had an impish grin. In future years, using his real name, he published three more novels and wrote a movie based on one of them; helped to found two magazines, *New York* and *The Institutional Investor*; lectured on economics at the Harvard Business School; served on corporate and collegiate boards ... it goes on and on. He is a connoisseur of wine, opera, and foreign policy; however, at Bragg he lived on a humbler level. While washing lightbulbs and polishing linoleum, he and I concocted the lyrics for two songs. One—we didn't get very far with it—was *The Chickenshit Mambo*:

> Mambo, mambo chickenshit,
> Mambo, mambo, chickenshit ...

We got farther with

> Psychological Warfare,
> More psycho than logical,
> We gotta lotta rumors,
> We gotta lotta bullshit,
> We gotta lotta lies.

At a 1963 meeting in Washington attended by generals and other representatives of the military-industrial complex, the chairman remarked, "If this group cannot bring about disarmament, then no one can," and a First RB&L alumnus (and then State Department member) named Richard J. Barnet laughed out loud. Barnet later helped to found the Institute for Policy Studies, an influential, left-leaning think tank that opposed the Vietnam War and tackled civil rights, environmental, and education issues. During the Johnson Administration, the FBI tapped the organization's phones; later, Barnet was on Nixon's "enemies list;" still later, the Institute was called "the Pluto of think tanks, the one farthest from the Reagan sun." Barnet, a Harvard Law School graduate, wrote fifteen books and many magazine articles; when I knew him, he was good company—and no better than the rest of us at picking up pine cones.

When he reached Ft. Bragg, Irving Lavin already had a Harvard PhD. He went on to become one of America's most distinguished art historians, writing many books on Roman and Florentine sculpture and architecture. For twenty-seven years, he was a professor at Princeton's Institute for Advanced Studies. Few of us Psywarriors managed to look gung-ho in our uniforms, but as I recall, Lavin looked particularly outlandish. He was relatively small, with horn-rimmed glasses and sharp, scholarly features; his stiff-peaked fatigue cap made him look (one of my mother's favorite expressions) like a mouse under a table.

* * *

On a few rare occasions, the smart, talented members of the battalion got assignments that actually used our professional experience. We taped a three-part radio program concerning the peaceful uses of atomic energy; the script wasn't bad, and the announcer, who later worked at a major network, sounded just like his hero, Edward R. Murrow. I suspect the battalion's commanding officer wanted the program so he could answer if anyone asked, "What can your people actually *do*?" We also produced leaflets urging soldiers to keep their canteens "spotlessly clean" and avoid drunken driving: "Christmas, the season of joy, can be violated by recklessness and stupidity on the highways." These were illustrated by our draftee commercial artists. The ambition of one artist was to design cars in Detroit; I believe he succeeded. Another artist was ordered to paint a mural in our commanding officer's office; as I recall, it showed paratroopers jumping out of planes. What our CO didn't realize was that the letters FTA—Fuck the Army—were hidden in choice spots.

Our most talented artist was likeable, mild-mannered James McMullan. He remembers a complex machine, bought at considerable expense from a nutty-professor inventor, which would supposedly print propaganda leaflets in several different languages. "The thing was a total farce," McMullan told me. "The officer in charge told us to stick it in the basement and never mention it again." After the Army, McMullan joined the celebrated Push Pin Studio design group, whose work was the first by Americans to be exhibited in the Louvre's Musée des Arts Décoratifs. Over the years, he did magazine illustrations, painted dozens of posters for New York's Lincoln Center Theater, and won five major artwork awards.

* * *

Besides these gifted draftees, the First RB&L included Regular Army enlistees. The service was their life, and in the end they'd get pensions. Some worked as cooks, truck drivers, or auto mechanics; most were "just plain sojers," content to follow any and all orders. These men came in several colors; some weren't exactly bright. I recall one guy who wouldn't wash himself, and had to be held under the shower by barracks-mates offended by his odor. I'd never spent time with men like these, and at first communication was tough, but then I heard their stories, and shared their daily experiences, and ate the same chow they did, and all of that built comradeship. I particularly remember dwarfish Corporal Morimoto, who was in his eighteenth year of service: "They keep busting me back to private when I get drunk—but so what?" Master Sergeant Taylor, from Georgia, got a pass to attend a murdered and dismembered relative's funeral and overstayed a week. Others would've been declared AWOL and punished; Taylor pulled some strings and his misdeed was forgotten. When one of us draftees succeeded in "bugging out"—for example, spending an hour at the PX instead of painting tree trunks—Taylor's inevitable greeting was, "Where ya bin, son?" In later, civilian years, whenever I and other RB&L alumni met, we asked that question.

Most of the time, the First RB&L's Regular Army soldiers behaved sensibly—but one evening, after the battalion had received high praise following a visit from the Inspector General, our officers rewarded all of us with a party. It was held in the Headquarters Company mess hall, which had been decorated with streamers and artwork. The officers came; we had piano, singing, a buffet supper, and countless kegs of beer. A fine party, and when it was over, there were three men in the hospital and one in the stockade. Some of the truck drivers got to fighting; a Korean War veteran threw a fit during which he saw Chinese Communists coming up a hill at him; and another guy tried to climb out of the latrine window, which was a good twenty feet off the ground. A great swarm of MPs surrounded our barracks, flourishing their rifles, and an especially drunken sojer perched on the roof, hurling insults down at them. When he finally came down, he dislocated his arm while crawling under the building.

* * *

All through my Army service, Sam Vaughan and Ken McCormick sent me new Doubleday books, and I spent some evenings reading. Other evenings, we scriptwriters worked on our own projects in the barracks-like office building (and Richard Mayer ran his stamp business). I wrote short stories on my Doubleday gift typewriter, and now I had an agent to send them to—Kay Ullman, who was working for Willis Kingsley Wing, one of the best in the business. Wing was gray-haired and middle-aged, but he had the muscular torso of a weightlifter: he'd had polio as a young man, and for years had heaved himself around on crutches.

Among my stories was one set in a village like Sakonnet, about a crotchety, elderly fisherman who saves a rich man's boat during a hurricane. One afternoon, when I was standing in the blazing-hot company street with my brass gleaming and my boots spit-shined, waiting for weapons inspection, an orderly room clerk brought me a telegram: *Woman's Day* magazine, which published famous authors, had bought the story for seven-hundred-and-fifty dollars, almost *ten times* my monthly pay of seventy-eight dollars!

Every writer recalls the elation of the first professional sale. I had only a moment to savor mine; then Sergeant Taylor cried, *"Ten-hut!"* and I snapped to attention and forced myself to become stone-faced. Second Lieutenant Marlin Flowers (the fool who'd had his wife check our toilet-cleaning) came slowly toward me. He stopped in front of me. I yanked my carbine off my shoulder and thrust it out. He grabbed it and squinted with one bulging eye down the barrel, searching eagerly for the tiniest speck of dust. All this time, my telegram shouted at me from my pocket and I wanted to bark with laughter and shout with joy.

I got through the inspection okay. A letter from Kay said that, to celebrate, she'd had champagne. Then Ken McCormick sent a congratulatory letter, saying, "I trust this is the first chapter of a novel you're going to write for Doubleday" and giving me his "affectionate best." In my story, the hero exclaimed, "Sweet American Jesus" (just like a real Sakonnet fisherman, Bill); in deference to their lady readers, the magazine's editors changed that to "Sweet America."

* * *

Ft. Bragg's noncommissioned officers had a club to escape to, a "good-ole-boys" bar and grill, and the commissioned officers had theirs, a fancier bar plus restaurant, with the choicest filet mignon at an astonishingly low price (a reward for their superior brains and achievements). The resort town of Southern Pines—with its rich retirees and many golf courses— was an hour's drive from our barracks, and five of us draftees rented a one-story, three-bedroom house for evenings and weekends. It cost almost nothing and we soon learned why: privately owned planes taking off deafeningly from the small Southern Pines airfield right next door narrowly missed tearing the roof off.

An aunt of Borden's, Elizabeth ("Buffie") Stevenson Ives, had a comfortable house in the fashionable part of town, and one evening invited all five of us for drinks. She looked a lot like her famous brother, and was handsomely dressed, as was her ex-diplomat husband. They were genial hosts, and a few days later Buffie called, inviting Borden, Gil Grosvenor, and me to dinner "to meet three lovely young women from the community."

Borden said, "Aunt Buffie, there are five of us sharing this house."

"I'm inviting you three," said Aunt Buffie.

The two who were left out were Jewish. Borden said to all of us, "I know what she's up to, but the three of us have to go, or she'll tell everyone in my family that I'm rude and ungrateful, and I'll never hear the end of it." Adlai Stevenson was divorced; if he'd become president, Aunt Buffie might have been, in effect, First Lady. The three young women weren't lovely, just boring, and we didn't see them again.

At Yale, I'd been visited a couple of times by a Protestant minister who urged me to go to Sunday services. The Army had chaplains of all faiths and I didn't want them seeking me out, so when I was first asked my religion, I said, "None." When our dog tags were issued, others carried the letters P, C, or J—but mine said Y. A few days later, I had to show my dog tags to a clerk who was filling out paperwork. He asked, "What's this Y for your religion?"

"It stands for 'None.'"

"Then it should be N."

"I know. Look—"

"Cut the bullshit, okay?"

I thought briefly, then said, "I'm a Yemenite." The clerk said, "Okay," and typed, "Yemenite." From then on, that was my religion.

My ghastliest job by far was a week of prisoner chasing. At 5:30 AM, a dozen of us were trucked to the Ft. Bragg stockade, a cluster of buildings surrounded by razor-wire-topped fences and overlooked by MPs in guard towers. Maybe a hundred prisoners were being drilled inside the fence—the idea was to keep them constantly busy, to exhaust them. They had white armbands sewn onto their fatigue uniforms, and weren't serious criminals; most had merely gone AWOL. All the same, they were frightening. Their drill field was small, so they did "the stockade shuffle:" all chanting cadence together—"*hut, taw, ha-ree, hore*"—the platoons took a full, right-foot step forward, then a left-foot half-step forward, the repeated in a syncopated, rocking limp, which had ferocious energy in it. At the command, "*Hah-ree, har!*" ("*To the rear, march!*"), the grim-faced, boot-thumping men whirled around as one. These guys were really good at this, and their primitive anger was terrifying.

As it turned out, these fierce fellows could be easily controlled. Most days, you followed two of them along one of the roads crisscrossing the two-hundred-square-mile Ft. Bragg reservation as they picked up litter. The hideous summer heat soon had them begging you to take them into the woods to cool off. We'd been warned that that could be dangerous. When you refused, some prisoners gave you a hard time, challenging you, testing your nerve: "Hey, man, you 'fraid o' sumpin'?" To silence them, you released the safety catch of your carbine and pointed it at them. Instantly, you were in command: could you be a homicidal maniac aching for a thrill? Prisoner chasing was agonizing physically and emotionally, and you sometimes felt sorry for your charges: when they weren't doing the stockade shuffle, they were a sad lot. But then there was the case of an over-sympathetic First RB&L artist-illustrator who gave in when his prisoners started pleading. Hidden among the trees, they jumped him, dismantled his carbine and scattered the pieces, stripped him naked, threw his uniform and boots up into the branches, and took off. The artist was court-martialed and reduced in rank; the prisoners were caught within days. Like almost all escapees, they'd simply gone home.

The Army Medical Corps fretted endlessly about VD, so every few weeks, around 3:00 AM, you'd be jolted awake by shouts of "Drop your cocks and grab your socks and hit the deck for pecker check!" Humiliation followed. I read somewhere that the First RB&L had Bragg's lowest VD rate. No wonder—we also had the highest percentage of twenty-one-year-old virgins. Naturally, we thought constantly about women. I sometimes stayed overnight with a welcoming faculty family at the University of North Carolina at Chapel Hill; when the softly treading, twenty-year-old daughter crept into my bedroom, I felt like a cad. (Earlier, at Ft. Dix, a fellow draftee named Peter Griffith offered me a lift to New York one weekend. The driver was his gorgeous, blonde wife, model-actress Tippi Hedren, later the star of Hitchcock's *The Birds* and the mother of Melanie Griffith. Flying toward the city in her sky-blue Cadillac convertible with the top down and the wind whipping my face—headed for a night with gentle, smiling Joan—was the only joyous moment in the misery of Basic Training.)

I was sometimes given jobs off-post; two were saddening, one maddening.

One evening, some of us eggheads were ordered to put on our steel helmets ("hemmets," Sergeant Taylor called them) and temporary Military Police armbands and go into Fayetteville to help actual MPs to round up noisy hordes of drunken paratroopers from the many bars and force them into trucks headed back to their barracks. I asked an MP what was going on and was told in bored tones, "It's payday." There must've been women who accommodated troopers on payday nights, but you never heard about them: Fayetteville was a quiet southern town with a church on damn near every corner. I once went to an evening revival meeting in a tent where, amidst hysterical "Alleluias," the Rev A. A. Allen laid his hands on sinners who then threw down their crutches.

In a dusty, backwoods town, I was part of a six-man honor guard at the burial of a World War II veteran. We rehearsed countless times: stand at attention, rifles at present arms; as the casket's being lowered and the bugler's blowing *Taps*, raise the rifles and fire volleys of blanks into the air. The mourners—all white—were dignified in their Sunday-go-to-meetin' clothes, and obviously poor. Afterwards, in the ramshackle American Legion clubhouse, we were given drinks and shoulder-thumps, and the widow and her undernourished children thanked us again and again. In the truck going back to Bragg, I thought, *Something's wrong with America if our sad little show is that family's grandest moment.*

The maddening incident came in the newsroom of the *Fayetteville Observer*, the local daily paper. Every week, half a dozen scriptwriters, in uniform, were trucked into town to put together a page of news from all over Ft. Bragg—awards, special operations, officers' social events. Obviously, the post's bosses felt we were the best qualified for the job. Working from notes from the various units—mainly the 82nd Airborne Division—we typed copy, took it into the pressroom, then edited the proofs. One week, a black scriptwriter—I forget his name—took in some pages. The presses were already running; their rumbling rhythm filled the building. Then, mysteriously, that sound slowly, slowly melted, then died entirely: the presses had been shut down. We stared at one another—what was wrong? In the weird silence, the pressroom boss—a white man, of course—strode out. "We don't start up again 'til that black man's outta there," he declared, "and don't ever send him back again." I repeat: that scriptwriter soldier was wearing a U.S. Army uniform.

* * *

In early June '55, Borden Stevenson and I drove his father to Northampton, Massachusetts. My sister was graduating from Smith College and Borden's father, who'd lost his '52 bid for the presidency and hadn't yet decided whether he'd try again, was giving the graduation address. We picked him and his aide, William McCormick Blair, up at a grand country house outside New York City. They were carrying briefcases, suitcases, and newspapers; I was struck by Stevenson's height and weight—photos had led me to expect a taller, leaner man.

We got under way, with Borden driving and me beside him. Suddenly, a cat darted out of a driveway. Borden braked hard, but the cat was motionless on the narrow road behind us.

A woman came out of the driveway, and Borden walked back and started to speak—but the woman said it wasn't his fault: she'd been trying to train the cat, but it often ran into the road. In the back seat, Stevenson had pulled his newspaper up to hide his face: he didn't want to be linked to pet tragedies—rotten publicity.

The drive resumed; we passed from back roads onto the highway. Outside Hartford, Connecticut, we stopped for lunch at a Howard Johnson's. While we waited to be seated, I was right behind Stevenson, and I saw people glance at him without recognizing him. We sat at a table against a wall. Stevenson was facing the room, studying the potential voters. No one was studying him. A waitress brought menus. She looked at Stevenson; to her, he was just another customer. His expression showed frustration, anxiety, and annoyance, and he began agitatedly drumming his fingers on the tabletop. Plainly, he was thinking, *If I'm this invisible, what chance do I have if I run again?* There were several moments of deep gloom ...

Then a man walked toward him, carrying a menu. As Stevenson dashed off his autograph, people turned to watch. Murmuring began: "It's Adlai Stevenson!" A few customers stood up and stared. The restaurant manager appeared, and shook Stevenson's hand. Others began approaching; within minutes, he was busy with handshakes and autographs. As we left, he was laughing merrily.

Now, it was my turn to drive and for Stevenson to sit beside me. We talked about how crazy and wasteful the First RB&L was. Stevenson kept urging me to drive faster: "I'm due at a reception at the college president's house!" The narrow highway was dangerous; as I sweated and clutched the steering wheel and dodged oncoming traffic, I kept thinking, *I may have the future of the world in my hands!* Finally, we were there, and Stevenson invited Borden and me to join the party.

As we all know, Stevenson ran again, and lost again. When that happened, I recalled a joke he'd made after his first loss: "Someone asked me how I felt and I said, 'Like a little boy who stubbed his toe in the dark. He said he was too old to cry and it hurt too much to laugh.'" I also recalled the ambition and anxiety that drove those drumming fingers.

* * *

The First RB&L had a "sister" unit on Smoke Bomb Hill: the 77th Special Forces Group, better known as the Green Berets; they were an elite, famous outfit whose wartime mission was to parachute behind enemy lines and train guerrillas in raiding supply and communication lines, ambushing convoys, and creating general mayhem. Many of the 77th's enlisted men were older than us draftees. They were from Iron Curtain countries, and had fought against Allied Forces during World War II, and had enlisted in the U.S. Army because five years of service would earn them U. S. citizenship. These were professional fighters; their name (and headgear) signified toughness and efficiency. Their commanding officer, Colonel Edson D. Raff, was a famed West Pointer who'd led the first American parachute jump in World War II, in Tunisia. Dwight Eisenhower called Raff's North African exploits "a minor epic ... the deceptions he practiced, the speed with which he struck, his boldness and aggressiveness, kept the enemy completely confused." I was once chosen to be his orderly for the day—which meant putting a blinding shine on my boots and driving him around in a Jeep. Although he'd fought in many bloody battles, he struck me as sensitive. Unfortunately, he was fanatical about appearances: visiting the Psychological Warfare library, he spotted some old newspapers he thought "unsightly," and had them burned. The papers were in Czech and Hungarian; Green Berets originally from those countries had worked hard to collect them so they could keep up their language skills. The only time I enjoyed sojerin' was when we Psywarriors marched with the 77th on Ft. Bragg's largest parade ground during evening flag-lowering ceremonies. Heart-stirring band music, the tramp of booted feet, the sight of the ultra-sharp, beautifully disciplined Green Berets striding along in unison just ahead—all of that gave me a thrill and created pride.

* * *

Starting in late October '55, I was one of one hundred and forty thousand GIs caught up in the largest Army maneuvers since World War II. For forty-five days, I lived in a tent in a swamp, wore a child's uniform, and pretended to make war.

Exercise Sage Brush took place on six million acres of Louisiana ground; almost two thousand tanks and twelve hundred aircraft were involved. It was intended, in the Army's words, to "test and develop nuclear-age division organizations and tactical concepts." Like all war games, it was carefully scripted (and, of course, only fake ammunition was used). The Aggressor forces, who had supposedly gained a foothold in the Gulf Coast area, would advance during the first few weeks; ultimately, they'd be defeated. Our battalion had been put on the losing side; to distinguish us from U.S. soldiers, we attached plastic ridges atop our helmets and wore bibs bearing the Aggressor emblem.

Our bivouac area was outside the tiny town of Ragley (which looked like its name). Getting there from Bragg in a many-miles-long convoy took five days. We rode in trucks, lying on our duffel bags, ate vile canned rations, and slept in pup tents. The journey's end was ten-man tents in a clearing in swampy woods. When it rained—and it rained a lot—hundreds of tiny frogs would appear and hop around on the tents' wooden floors. Tom Riha and I ate a not-too-bad Thanksgiving dinner together off mess trays half filled with rainwater. One weekend, six of us drove overnight to Monterey, Mexico. The hotel rooms, with bathtubs you could soak in all day, were ludicrously cheap, as were dinner in the city's best (French) restaurant and a visit to a wonderful bordello: a vast courtyard under brilliant stars with a mariachi band, delicious cerveza, delicious señoritas. I agree, I agree, prostitution's evil; but if you'd told me that then, my response would've been merely a satisfied sigh.

I kept some of the leaflets we produced on our mobile presses during Sage Brush; they're painfully sophomoric. Designed to persuade "enemy" (U.S.) forces to surrender, they contained vague messages like, "Powerful Aggressor forces are in your rear. Your situation is hopeless. You have suffered many hardships. Now is your chance to escape from further privation." One showed a half-naked girl on a bed; the text started "HOW LONG HAS IT BEEN ... since you've had a good night's sleep?" Another said, "Your hidden enemy SUMAC. It's all around you, poison sumac, waiting to contaminate and torture ..."

There were actual dangers facing the U.S. forces, which we tried to use as propaganda, but the brass wouldn't let us. One danger was small, colorful coral snakes, whose bite could be lethal. I saw several dead ones, hung on fences to remind soldiers to shake out their boots before putting them on. When we suggested a scary snakebite leaflet, we were told we couldn't get too serious about Sage Brush's negatives. Then, in a local newspaper, we found a short, grim piece reporting—truthfully—that two U.S. soldiers, dozing on the ground at night in sleeping bags, had been fatally run over by a tank: squashed flat amid screams and great jets of blood. We photocopied the article and added, "Don't Let This Happen to You—Surrender!" Our commanding officer took one look at the layout and said, "you want to print leaflets saying two guys got squashed by a tank? If just *one* soldier's mother got just *one* of those leaflets and sent it to her congressman, Exercise Sage Brush would be finished!"

While our unit was forbidden to do an effective job, our Smoke Bomb Hill colleagues, the Green Berets, were merrily proving their worth again and again by sneaking across supposedly heavily guarded U.S. lines at night. They stole food and misdirected ammunition convoys. They plastered trucks and tanks with stickers saying, "This has been destroyed by the 77th Special Forces." A lieutenant general named Adams woke one morning to find YOU ARE DEAD written in lipstick on his blanket. A National Guard colonel discovered a lipstick stripe on his neck, indicating that his throat had been slit from ear to ear. These antics weren't in Sage Brush's script, so the Green Berets were sent home.

* * *

Back on Smoke Bomb Hill, I was promoted to Specialist Third Class, and my countdown-'til-release continued. When the glorious day arrived, I was given two hundred dollars as mustering-out pay and awarded the National Defense Services Medal (I wasn't presented with an actual *medal*, just a piece of paper saying that the decoration had been authorized). The day before I bid my friends farewell, I was given one last menial job: sweeping up the blood-soaked sawdust on the floor of the Ft. Bragg meat processing plant. This was a vast, one-story concrete building. The temperature inside was around forty-five. Railroad cars arrived outside and headless, hoofless, blood-dripping carcasses were shoved into the building, dangling on hooks from an overhead track. Roughly twenty gore-spattered Army butchers, wielding enormous knives, sliced off particular hunks, then pushed the carcasses along to the next butchers, who sliced off *their* particular hunks; it was a gruesomely efficient disassembly line. The butchers wore Middle Ages-looking chain mail aprons and finger guards; one told me, "You never know when your knife hand's gonna slip." By the track's end, the carcasses were skeletons; by the day's end, I was one, too.

Nine

THE TESTOSTERONE-TINTED WINDOW

Back at Doubleday, I got a warm welcome in the editorial department. I brought Jerry Goodman's second novel—about a young American girl's year in Paris—to Ken McCormick; he accepted it happily, but then Goodman hated the jacket photo. (Ken: "He wants the whole first printing re-jacketed! No way!") The book was ultimately published to okay reviews. I wanted to continue in editorial, but the sales promotion department was shorthanded, so I was sent there to write press releases, jacket copy, and catalogues. A Billy Graham underling and I worked on getting the reverend's message across in a book jacket's limited space; I've never met anyone so unctuous. I also worked with the yachtsman and all-around bon vivant Gerard Lambert; his memoir was a delight, and so was he. He'd made millions by bringing the word "halitosis" into the American language (his family owned the company that made Listerine), and he was the direct opposite of Billy's sanctimonious flack: to him, flim-flamming was glorious fun. My jacket copy for a Brendan Gill novel was (unintentionally) cliché-ridden, and Gill, with typical vitriol, asked his editor, Clark Potter, "What moron wrote this?" During the next few months, I hunted for clichés in Gill's *New Yorker* writings; Clark reported that Gill wasn't pleased when he was shown my collection.

I was hoping to get back to editing—and was writing in my spare time—when I got lucky again: Doug Kennedy, a slightly older Sakonnet friend who'd recently become Editor in Chief of *True* ("The Man's Magazine") offered me a job as an Associate Editor, with a slightly larger paycheck.

True, a monthly with a tone both cheesy and classy and a circulation of over two million, published pieces on hunting, fishing, adventure, male historical figures, notable living men, men's clothing, and related subjects, plus male-oriented opinion pieces, humorous anecdotes, and cartoons (and, in keeping with its title, no fiction). It's been called a "testosterone-tinted window into a world defined by guns, sports, war, politics, crime, and history." Many of its screeds were sexist; if published today, they'd evoke hysterical laughter. At the time, I occasionally winced—but the job was a thousand times better than grinding out sales copy. *True's* main competitor was *Argosy*; *Playboy* emphasized sex, so was in a different category. *True* ran some mild cheesecake, but never any nude centerfolds; its editorial pitch was, "You're an outdoorsy guy, livin' in your own world; readin' *True* is like sittin' at a campfire, drinkin' beer with your buddies and swappin' yarns; forget the pesky women-folk." That philosophy served *True* well for three decades (born in 1937, it died in 1968), but sex sells better: *Playboy* is still with us.

True paid writers and illustrators well. Some of its articles had strange titles: *Luigi, the Battleship Killer* (about a famed 1917 torpedo boat captain); *Build Yourself a Seagoing Station Wagon* (how to construct a houseboat); and *Out Where There's Room to Rope a Roar* (lassoing mountain lions in the Rockies). *True* was one of several magazines put out by Fawcett Publications—they also had *True Confessions, Mechanix*

Illustrated, and others, plus the profitable book operations Gold Medal and Crest, which released the work of John D. MacDonald, Kurt Vonnegut, MacKinlay Kantor, Louis L'Amour, and others. In its scope and earnings, Fawcett was kind of the magazine-pulp book equivalent of Doubleday—without Doubleday's distinguished backlist and (usually) better taste.

Fawcett Publications, Inc. was born in 1919 in Minnesota, when Wilford Hamilton Fawcett, a First World War veteran, put out *Captain Billy's Whiz Bang*, a twenty-five-cent collection of smutty jokes. Wilford wrote a monthly editorial, "Drippings from the Fawcett," in which he called his wife "the henna-haired heckler" and himself "this bristle-whiskered old sod buster." After *Whiz Bang* came such publications as *Battle Stories, Screen Secrets,* and *Smokehouse Monthly.* In the 1930s, the company's magazines had a combined monthly circulation of ten million. By the time I got to *True*, Captain Billy had—as he might have put it—long since gone to his reward and his four rich sons were running the company. In the luxurious penthouse of the company's West Forty-Fourth Street office building, drinks were reportedly dispensed through the gold penis of a nude statue. I can't confirm that: the Fawcett boys never honored me with an invitation.

Doubleday's editorial offices were sedate and posh; *True*'s featured shirt sleeves, worn linoleum floors, fluorescent lights, cramped cubicles, far younger staffers, and lots of bustle, particularly on Thursdays, when cartoonists visited with sketches that they hoped would be green-lighted. Half a dozen might be seated outside the cartoon editor's cubicle, talking shop and entertaining one another; it reminded me of the artists' parties at the Whitney Museum. I got to know a couple of the cartoonists, and was especially fond of shy, quiet Bill O'Brian. A five-part drawing of O'Brian's showed a depressed-looking businessman walking toward a mirror. As he passes it, he sees a reflection of Abraham Lincoln. He halts. He thinks. Back at the mirror, he sees his own reflection.

Many of the cartoonists who contributed to *True* were well-known: Herbert Goldberg, Lee Lorenz, Charles Dedini, Chon Day. The slant was mostly macho. A woman with an extra- large derriere says to another woman, "I don't believe in getting mad when a man pinches me—I just turn the other cheek." A man, coming home to find his house ransacked by burglars and his wife bound and gagged, says to her, "I suppose this means dinner will be late again!" In an obstetrician's office, an obviously well-off, older woman says to a young woman in a maid's uniform, "Good Heavens, Gertrude, what are *you* doing here?" *True* had a special arrangement with Virgil (Vip) Partch and ran his cartoons regularly. Oddly, they were seldom macho: as their dog riding a bicycle races after a sedan, a woman says to her husband, "I thought you taught him not to chase cars."

Doug Kennedy had been the Sports Editor of *Time* and the skipper of a PT boat in the war. He liked racing sports cars; in one Monte Carlo Rally, his car flipped over (he wasn't hurt). In addition to him, *True* had Managing, Art, Supervising, and Outdoors Editors, plus seven Associate Editors. Most Associates were married, and lived modestly; some commuted from the suburbs; none had ever killed a battleship or roped a roar. One of the Associates, Richard, had a serious drinking problem. Chuckling at the memory, he told us that one night he'd been locked up in Bellevue Hospital's drunk ward. "They wouldn't let me out," Richard said. "They'd taken away most of my clothes, but not my cigarette lighter. I set a blanket on fire and threw it out a window and in the confusion, I escaped down the emergency stairs half-naked."

The Associate Editors I got to know best were both named Bill. The first was a lively, funny Texan who was married to a dark-haired, funny Norwegian and used to give parties built around his marvelous chili (he later published a fine book about the Lafayette Escadrille). The second Bill—tall and moody—had fought in brutal Pacific battles as a Marine Corps major; he never discussed the battles, but plainly he'd been deeply affected. Ironically, this Bill edited the humor page and chose the cartoons. For a time, he'd worked for Walt Disney as an animator; later, he'd earned a meager living as a cartoonists' "idea man." He said he used to ride alone for hours on the top deck of a Fifth Avenue bus while trying to come up with funny situations—and that was the hardest work in the world.

Young, pretty Polly was *True*'s only female Associate Editor. She was the assistant to the Outdoors Editor, and knew as much as he did about pheasant-shooting and fly-fishing and all the rest. So that *True*'s male readers wouldn't learn her gender, on the masthead, her first name was "P." She shared an apartment with Fred, an editor at another Fawcett magazine, *Cavalier*. They had a poodle named Fenner, who had four siblings—Merrill, Lynch, Pierce, and Bean. At home during the cocktail hour, Polly used to put Fenner on her lap and trim his coat with nail scissors. Fred believed strongly in tradition, and one Christmas insisted that Polly cook a goose for dinner. She did it reluctantly ("It's very labor-intensive"). Guests were expected; to brighten the room, she hung a jazzy Christmas mobile above the dining table. Fred walked in, hated the mobile, snatched it down, and flung it out their fifth-floor window into the backyard (Fawcett editors loved defenestration). Polly marched into the kitchen, returned with the goose, and flung *it* out. They both left the apartment (separately). When they returned several days later, the goose's bones were lying in the backyard, picked clean by alley cats.

As the newest, youngest Associate Editor, I did many different jobs. I corrected proofs; wrote illustration captions and article titles and subtitles; and read the slush pile, a task as wearisome as at Doubleday—but I did find a few publishable pieces. My biggest job was editing. *True*'s policy was, writers didn't get to see changes in their copy before it went to press unless they insisted. Because of space limitations, we sometimes made sizable cuts, and we routinely changed wording. This was interesting work—it wasn't that far from actual writing—but it was time-consuming. I often took manuscripts home, so I had few chances to do short stories; I did sell a couple of them to (frankly) lesser magazines.

* * *

Once I'd settled in, I began to take pride in some of *True*'s articles. During its twenty-fifth anniversary in 1962, *True* published an anthology containing forty of those articles, going back to 1949. There were pieces by C. S. Forester on the frigate *Constitution,* by Jimmy Breslin on the jockey Earl Sande, by Barnaby Conrad on the matador Joselito, and by Aldous Huxley on what the world might look like in 1986 (when a fiftieth anniversary anthology might be published). Other writers on the table of contents included John Dos Passos, Philip Wylie, Bob Considine, John Lardner, James Ramsey Ullman, Paul Gallico, and W. C. Heinz. When Heinz died in 2008, almost half of his long *New York Times* obituary consisted of excerpts from two famous articles he wrote for *True.*

Those authors are impressive; but shouldn't the world's greatest man's magazine have published the work of the world's manliest, most famous writer—Ernest

Hemingway? Well, *True* did once—and then there was the big one that got away.

Fawcett's editorial director was Ralph Daigh, a middle-aged, well-liked, modest-sized man with an immodest-sized ego. In 1950, he paid Hemingway $3,700 (a hefty sum then) for a piece about hunting pronghorn antelope in Idaho, which *True* ran even though it wasn't good. Later that year, a bearded Hemingway strode into Daigh's office and said he was willing to do more— what did *True* want? In a 1977 book, Daigh said he replied, "Write a story about a sport you like most. Write it in such a way that it will excite the reader— permit him to live the experience. We want a *story*, not an article."

Hemingway said he had an idea, but the piece would be long—about ten thousand words.

Daigh asked what the subject might me.

"Fishing for blue marlin. A great true story. How much will you pay?"

Although he knew he was straining *True*'s budget, Daigh replied, "A dollar a word. Ten thousand dollars."

The two shook hands. Several weeks later, Hemingway phoned. The story was running long; how much would *True* pay for a piece that might be thirty thousand words? Still a dollar a word?

True's policy was, no serials: the story had to fit into a single issue. Daigh said, "Send it when it's finished. We'll make an offer when we see how much of it we can publish."

Hemingway replied, "It would be impossible to cut this story."

"On September 1, 1952," Daigh wrote, "*Life* magazine published a thirty-thousand-word 'novel' by Ernest Hemingway in one issue entitled *The Old Man and The Sea* ... It was published in hard-cover ... and attracted worldwide attention ... It is Hemingway's biggest-selling novel, won the Pulitzer Prize for

Literature, and contributed hugely to his being awarded the Nobel Prize.

"We got no more work from Ernest."

* * *

Every month, the magazine's last page, titled "This Funny Life," ran true, humorous anecdotes submitted by readers. *True* paid one hundred dollars for published anecdotes, so hundreds arrived. I took my turn reading them. It was a tiresome job because most were badly written or simply not funny—but at least they were genuine, and sometimes touching: someone was trying to communicate, to say, "Share my life." Others were flagrant lies: perhaps in bars, or barbershops, readers heard freshly minted jokes, and they sent them in, saying, "This happened to me." Some of these larcenous souls enclosed detailed letters spelling out their honesty. One particular story, involving a nun and a gas station air hose, came from a retired Admiral ("I'm an Annapolis graduate"), then from a small-town businessman ("I'm the president of our Chamber of Commerce"). Normally, submissions weren't returned, but this time I sent the businessman's story and covering letter to the Admiral and vice-versa, with notes saying, "You two should get acquainted."

For many years, *True* had published excerpts from books. Doug Kennedy wanted more of them; perhaps because I'd worked for a book publisher, I was chosen to search for possibilities. A letter went out and dozens of "fresh-off-the-presses" volumes and galley proofs began flooding in. The bookshelf in my cubicle was soon jam-packed. One evening when I was working late, I returned from the men's room to find a fellow-editor loading a suitcase with books I'd read and found unusable.

"Don't you know that selling these to secondhand dealers is an editorial perk?" he asked, exiting with his spoils.

From then on, I loaded up my own suitcase.

Rumor said that Errol Flynn's autobiography, *My Wicked, Wicked Ways*, was great entertainment, and was sure to be a bestseller. The book's publisher was so concerned that the juicy bits might be leaked that I had to go to their office and read the galleys in a room with the door closed. *True* paid a lot for a long excerpt. A few years later, Flynn's ghostwriter admitted that some of the most colorful parts—for example, the description of young Errol castrating lambs with his teeth in the Australian outback—were fake.

The advertisements in *True* were masculine: "It takes a tough blade to shave a tough beard;" "Women say 'deodorant.' Men say 'Trig.'" Liquor ads were everywhere, plus cigar and cigarette ads, with celebrities selling their names and faces: "This Christmas, Jack Benny is giving (yes, giving!) cartons of Luckies to a few close friends. Why don't you?" On its own ad pages, *True* ran ads advertising its ad pages:

> It IS a man's world ... Untruths have been quoted to advertisers about the importance of women as purchasers. Truth is, the man's decision to buy is the *most* important ...*True* is the largest selling man's magazine in the world. Bigger than *Time*, bigger than *Newsweek*. More than 2,300,000 copies per issue.

* * *

I moved into a small furnished apartment on West Fifty-Fifth Street, between Fifth and Sixth Avenues. My rent was low in this high-rent district because I had to move out for six weeks every year so the owners could come into town for Thanksgiving and Christmas. There were two bedrooms, so I shared the rent with Nick, my "Greek god" friend from Loomis. After Amherst and Army service in (postwar) Korea, Nick had become the unit manager of the Huntley-Brinkley news program, one of the greatest in TV history (he didn't talk about greatness, but simply said, "I carry a clipboard and make sure they're in their seats when the cameras go on"). For a time, Nick and the actress Joan Hackett were together.

The apartment next door belonged to Selene Walters, a slightly older, great-looking blonde who'd played small parts in Hollywood movies. She invited us for drinks several times. Her place was beautifully scented; she was warm and funny; we agreed that she was the ideal neighbor. We began noticing that she had frequent male visitors at all hours; I once rode up in the elevator with her and the actor George Sanders, who plainly didn't like being seen with her. In 1991, there was a great-to-do when Kitty Kelley wrote that in the early 1950s, Ronald Reagan had raped Selene. Kelley said that the two met in a Hollywood nightclub. She gave him her address and he came calling at 3:00 AM. Kelley quoted Selene as saying, "He forced me on the couch ... It was the most pitched battle I've ever had, and suddenly in a matter of seconds I lost ... They call it date rape today." Selene later told another writer that she bore Reagan no ill will, and even voted for him.

Nick had been hoping for many years to sail around the world. Finally, his chance came. As I recall, a friend of his built a boat somewhere on the West Coast and they started from there. Nick moved all of his belongings out of the apartment except for his set of the *Encyclopedia Britannica*; he said he'd pick that up in a few years, when he got back. He hoped to write a book about his adventures. Many months later, he wrote that the trip was over, and he was living in the Bahamas and had a radio program where he played the guitar and sang. The next thing I learned was that he'd drowned while scuba diving. He's buried in the Bahamas; I gave his *Encyclopedia* to his brother, Peter (who started the South Street Seaport). I think often about Nick. He was the best possible company; he had humor and imagination and spirit; he had already accomplished a lot, and would have accomplished more. As someone said about the poet Hart Crane, he was "an unfinished romantic."

* * *

When Nick moved out of the apartment, Borden moved in. The first day, he said, "If my mother calls, I'm not here." (Borden's mother had mental problems.) Through Borden, I met people I might not have met otherwise, including Gay and Nan Talese, Toots Shor, and Sammy Davis Jr., who took us night-clubbing and praised Borden's father nonstop in showbiz argot. Another evening, Leonard Lyons showed us the clubs *he* favored. The actor Robert Evans and the luscious actress Gia Scala came to a cocktail party we gave; sadly, I can't recall a word they said (they probably spoke showbiz argot, too).

Into my apartment with Borden came an attractive English girl—I think her name was Felicity. Borden's father was now practicing law in New York. One evening, Borden, Felicity, and I had a dozen people in for a spaghetti dinner. They ate in the living room; when they left, sauce-stained plates and silverware, overflowing ashtrays, soiled napkins, and lipstick-smeared glasses were scattered on the mantelpiece, the windowsills, the bookcases, and the coffee table. We were too tired to clean up, and agreed to do it together the next evening, when we got home from work.

I was the first to arrive. A minute later, the doorbell rang—and there, looking distinguished and lawyerly, was Adlai Stevenson, asking, "Is Bordie here?"

I said he'd probably be home soon.

Stevenson asked if he could come in: "I'd like to see where Bordie lives."

In the living room, he gazed around wordlessly. "It's not," I said, "always like this."

In Borden's bedroom, Felicity's underwear and stockings were strewn about. This was before shacking-up was routine; Stevenson's eyebrows rose.

Back in the living room, he said he'd wait for a few minutes in hopes of seeing Borden. He moved the dishes off a chair; I got him a drink.

We sat surrounded by squalor. Now I had a real problem. From our previous meetings, I'd sensed that he was an intellectual snob, a decent, somewhat distant man not interested in small talk; what could I possibly say that would intrigue him? I was struggling, and Stevenson's eyes were glazing over, when I heard the front door open. I prayed it was Borden: father and son could chat, and then father would leave. If it was Felicity, things might be awkward.

It *was* Felicity—and things went beautifully. Borden had told me that his father relished the company of attractive women; now, he turned on the flirtation, and Felicity shot flirtation right back. The minutes sped by; then Stevenson squeezed her hand and departed. Ten minutes later, Borden arrived, and the cleanup began.

* * *

Noël Favrelière was short and slight, with a strong nose and short-cropped brown hair. He was four years younger than I, and had been born in La Rochelle, France; his family was in the hotel business. He had a heavy accent; his English was workable, but not great. From the start, he intrigued me—I'd never met a man who, because he'd saved another man's life, had been condemned to death.

Noël had done two years of compulsory service in the French Army, then had been recalled: the French were trying to put down the rebellion in Algeria. In 1956, he was stationed in the desert near the mountains where the rebels had their camps. On the evening of August 26th, he was given a prisoner to guard and was told that the next morning the prisoner would be helicoptered up over the mountains and pushed out— something that was done often. "I couldn't let that happen," Noël said, "so that night I released him. And that meant I had to go with him."

Noël and the prisoner made their way into the mountains where Noël was greeted as a hero. Later, there were reports that he fought against the French; he swore to me that he didn't. The rebels got him into Tunisia; in the spring of '57, he came to New York, where he had a minor job in an industrial design firm. Meantime, a French military court sentenced him to death.

I met Noël through my Army friend Chris Bird. He thought Noël's story—which Noël had already started to write—might interest *True*, or a book publisher; could I help? I liked Noël a lot: he was shy and quiet, but you could sense great strength. He was a man without a country—he couldn't go home without risking death, yet his attitude was, "I can live with that." "The best thing I've done," he said, "is to desert."

We worked in my apartment in our spare time, finally producing a manuscript in English titled *The Desert at Dawn. True* passed on it; so did book editors: "Americans aren't interested in the Algerian War." In November of '58, Noël and I dined at my parents' apartment; his thank-you note said:

Chère Madame, I would like to tell you how much, the exile that I am, had enjoyed your wonderful Thanksgiving dinner and had appreciated your graciousness towards him. I hope you'll excuse my deplorable English grammar. Very truly yours ...

After a few months, I began to hear less and less from Noël; he seemed to have disappeared. Several years later (I think in 1967), he sent me a copy of his book. It had been published in France (in French) in '60. According to a French newspaper, every intellectual in the country (many of them Communists) knew his story. Starting in '63, he returned to France using aliases. "I had tons of papers," he told a reporter. "I lived with five or six identities." He received a pardon in February '66; in '67, the Renault auto company hired him as an executive. He married, had children, prospered, and through the years has been celebrated by many of his countrymen.

I spent many of my after-work hours in midtown, not far from my apartment. The Whitney Museum had moved into a new building, on West Fifty-Fourth Street, in the Museum of Modern Art's garden; I went to openings and exhibitions. (The Whitney moved to Seventy-Fifth Street in 1966.) Public relations people sent *True* invitations to book-launchings, brand-launchings, auto shows, boat shows; some were lively. At one party, John McCarten, *The New Yorker*'s movie critic, blathered on about "that" and "which:" if you didn't know the precise difference between them, you were stupid. According to a man who knew him well, McCarten was "kind of a Humphrey Bogart character—tough, outside, but sweet inside. He said things like, 'That guy has an ass like an Armenian whore!'"

I spent many evenings with Bodie Neilsen, a tall, blonde, striking-looking, Danish-born Vassar graduate, but I had the wisdom not to accompany her to the writers' poker games where she often came out a winner. Part of Bodie's great appeal was her intelligence: she worked as a magazine editor, and while still in college, she had a long article published in *The New York Times Magazine*. Some days, when we both had evening engagements, we went to my apartment at lunchtime. In Sakonnet, after a moonlight stroll on the beach, she insisted with typical whimsicality that we sleep all night in the dunes. I had to mention many negatives—sand fleas, mosquitoes, possible rain—to coax her back into my car. Later, Bodie lived with Irwin Shaw for eight stormy, glamorous years; she said he asked her to marry him, but she refused, partly because of his heavy drinking. They met at a 1967 dinner party where Bodie was offered a chance to sit beside either Shaw or Frank Sinatra; believing he'd be more interesting, she chose the creator over the crooner. I got to know Bodie's equally alluring roommate, Karen Gundersen, who was also proposed to by a celebrated man, *My Fair Lady*'s lyricist, Alan Jay Lerner; unlike Bodie, Karen said yes.

* * *

Jerry Goodman got married. The reception was held at the posh River Club; two of the bride's pals, Lenny and Steve (that's Bernstein and Sondheim) played the piano and sang for us. After "Where ya bin, son?" I said to Goodman, "This is a long way from Smoke Bomb Hill." Frank Platt, a Dalton friend, got married in upper New York State. I was an usher and shared a motel room with Ivan Chermayeff, another usher. The evening before the wedding, Ivan slipped on the edge of a swimming pool and broke his collarbone. The next morning, I had the unwelcome task of helping a man wearing an enormous cast to get dressed, top to toe, in wedding finery. After the reception in the bride's grand house, all ten ushers went to a bedroom where Frank changed clothes. At one point, three of us were asked to leave the room. We weren't members of Harvard's Porcellian Club—all the others were. I heard that during our banishment, Frank had messages for his bride painted in iodine on his belly, but he denied it.

Near *True*'s offices, there were first-class, cheap restaurants, notably the Blue Ribbon, where you could watch *The New Yorker*'s brilliant A. J. Liebling adding to his girth. Everywhere in the city, there were wonderful bars smelling of ale, cigars, and hamburgers with onions. Many bars were run by Irishmen: P. J. Clarke's, Daly's, Glennon's, Tim Costello's (with Thurber drawings on the walls and sometimes nearly blind Thurber himself teetering on a bar stool). Irish bars were where you met your friends; they were to New York what cafés were to Paris, and New York is far poorer since they closed. One bar, on upper Madison Avenue, offered a unique advantage: next door was a hotel that rented rooms by the hour. Another bar was in the apartment of my Doubleday friend Clark Potter. Formerly a linen closet, it had shelves for bottles and glasses, and the walls were papered with Clark's father's worthless, 1929 stock certificates.

Downtown, Greenwich Village was remote, picturesque, and unspoiled by today's hordes. On misty nights, you walked down narrow streets in a trafficless hush: soft lights in parlor windows; solitary dog walkers; you almost expected to hear a bell-ringing town crier: "Midnight, and all's well!" On Hudson Street was perhaps the most famous bar in the city, the White Horse Tavern. I went there with beautiful Natalie ("Natasha") Edgar, who had wonderful eyes: when she was amused, they shone with laughter. Natasha was very smart and a talented painter, and lived near the White Horse up four steep flights of stairs. Lust flew me up those stairs—until I blundered. One weekend, on the beach in Sakonnet, I found a gorgeous white seagull feather. Thinking that Natasha would love its looks, I mailed it to her. She was furious: didn't I know that white feathers were signs of cowardice? What had I meant by sending it? Where was our relationship going? Natasha later married the successful sculptor Philip Pavia, who was twenty years older, and had two sons. She wrote often for *ARTnews* and continued to paint, ultimately having ten solo shows.

At the White Horse Tavern, everyone seemed to worship the fact that Dylan Thomas had drunk himself to death there. I had some strange talks there with Alex Trocchi, a Scottish novelist who lived on a scow on the Hudson River. In Paris, he had edited an avant-garde magazine called *Merlin*, which published Henry Miller, Samuel Beckett, and Pablo Neruda, among others. Alex was gaunt, brilliant, and (I didn't know it then) a heroin addict. He sometimes behaved criminally: during a TV debate on drug use, he injected himself on camera. He was on bail at the time, charged with giving heroin to a minor, and it seemed certain he'd go to jail, but with the help of friends (among them Norman Mailer), Trocchi made it over the Canadian border.

At a Greenwich Village cocktail party where no one injected themselves, I met tall, ultra-WASPish George Plimpton—who knew Alex Trocchi and had served on *Merlin*'s editorial board. I was awed by Plimpton because of his *Paris Review* work; in person, he was funny and sympathetic. We happened to leave the party at the same time; in the elevator, he asked if I'd like to see a colorful bar nearby, on Minetta Lane. It was called Romero's: sawdust on the floor, a jukebox, lots of what were then called beatniks (one of them, Jack Kerouac, described the bar as "the greatest"). The main attraction was the handsome, Puerto Rican, laid-back-but-attention-grabbing host, Johnny Romero. Standing behind the bar, he would set a glass of brandy on fire, dip his finger into the flame, pull it out coated with blazing liquid, and extinguish it in his mouth. Very effective—lots of "Oohs" and "Ahs." I later got to know Romero better, under bizarre circumstances.

In addition to Trocchi, Plimpton had another British lawbreaker friend, Frank Norman, who spent three years in prison in England for minor crimes and was the author of the prize-winning play-with-music *Fings Ain't Wot They Used T'Be*. At a party at Plimpton's famous 72nd Street apartment, Norman and I were talking when he suddenly clamped his arms around my waist, said something like, "Here's a game I played in jail," and tried to stuff the seat of my trousers up my rear end with his finger. It took a moment to throw him off; I realized later that I should've stopped him by trying to rip his ear off (incidentally, he wasn't homosexual). Learning that he'd had a psyche-warping childhood (abandoned by his mother, raised in state institutions) made me sympathetic—for ten seconds. Fights weren't uncommon at Plimpton's parties: once he had to break one up between Norman Mailer and Harold Humes, the brilliant, sandy-haired, meerschaum-pipe-smoking author of the novels *The Underground City* and *Men Die*.

Some people think that Plimpton started the *Paris Review* single-handedly. In fact, Peter Matthiessen, Humes, and others created it; Plimpton was invited to become editor. I got to know Humes, and like his many other friends was saddened by the paranoia that began showing in his early thirties. He once spent a night with my wife Patty and me in New York. At the start of dinner, he was cheery and full of interesting talk. Halfway through, he began mentioning "*Them*—the men who're spying on me." During dessert, he told us agitatedly that "they" had planted radios in his teeth so "they" could learn how much he knew about America's military secrets. He went to bed still haunted by "them." In the morning, he was gone, leaving us a poem thanking us for our hospitality; it was sensitive, emotional, and completely sane.

* * *

Around the time when George Plimpton took me to Johnny Romero's, a lonely woman in Edith and Lloyd's apartment building, bent on suicide, turned on her gas stove without lighting it. An hour later, sparks from defective wiring caused a horrendous explosion, knocking the kitchen wall down on Mr. Marshall, a well-dressed, well-spoken, elderly eccentric who was sleeping in the next apartment. Firemen took the woman to the morgue and Mr. Marshall to the hospital. The next day, lightly bandaged, Mr. Marshall was seated in the downstairs lobby, proclaiming, "So inconsiderate! All she needed was a dollar's worth of sleeping pills!"

* * *

One of my jobs at *True* was editing pieces by redheaded, always-infectiously laughing Bill Ballentine, a writer-cartoonist who'd trouped with a circus as a clown, designer, and publicist. Bill told—and wrote and illustrated—wonderful stories about circus life and was a great lunch and cocktail-hour companion. He gave me a copy of his fascinating circus book, *Wild Tigers and Tame Fleas*, which he inscribed, "To Dave, who has the patience of an elephant." On the end papers, he'd drawn cartoons. One showed an elephant staring anxiously over his shoulder at a moronic-looking handler who was carrying a rake and saying to another handler, "Di'n' ja say ya wuz gonna learn me how to rake a elephant?" In the book, Bill explained that before performing, circus elephants were forced to empty their bowels by rearing repeatedly on their hind legs. If that didn't work, "The elephant man performs a decidedly unpleasant operation known as 'raking,' plunging his bare arm into the elephant."

The higher-ups ordered *True* to publish a Canadian edition containing extra pages of Canadian-oriented articles and ads. They told me to find the articles. Again, letters went out—to Canadian literary agents, publishers, and writers' groups. We began to realize that we had to put an actual Canadian in charge. Farley Mowatt, one of Canada's most popular authors, who had written about his war service and his work as a naturalist, agreed to come for a talk. He and his New York agent—one of the best in the business—arrived an hour late, after lunch. Mowatt could obviously tolerate liquor and made sense, but the agent stretched himself out on a couch and snored loudly. A deal was ultimately made, but the Canadian edition lasted only a short while (not enough ads, as I recall).

* * *

Cavalier, another Fawcett publication, had its offices in the same building. The two were aimed at pretty much the same readers, but *Cavalier* published fiction and was less sexist and more iconoclastic—for example, calling Frank Sinatra and his Rat Pack

> a gaggle of overpaid and underdone characters—one of the more grisly phenomena of our time ... Dean Martin is a natural-born head waiter ... Sammy Davis Jr. makes the mistake of confusing energy with talent ... Peter Lawford: in every group there has to be someone to send out for coffee.

Cavalier sold for twenty-five cents, versus *True*'s thirty-five; on its cover was, "This magazine guaranteed or double your money back." The editors included Fred, the mobile-flinger mentioned earlier and Richard Suskind, later notorious for helping Clifford Irving to concoct his fraudulent Howard Hughes "autobiography" (another *Cavalier* coworker recalls Suskind as a capable editor and an "engaging rascal" and says his impoverished Bronx childhood—"Dick's family moved whenever the rent came due"—may have fueled his misdeeds). Arthur Herzog, the author of several books including a bestselling novel about killer bees, *The Swarm*, also helped to edit *Cavalier*. Its budget was smaller than *True*'s, but they published first-rate writers, and the editors felt they earned their (unofficial) slogan, "The magazine that's too good to be *True*." One particular bit of *Cavalier* ingenuity propelled its staff into grand company. The editor, Bob Curran, spotted a newspaper item about an Australian named Reg Evans who was a coastwatcher in August 1943—one of the officers, native islanders, and escaped prisoners of war who observed enemy movements in the Pacific and rescued stranded Allied servicemen. Evans, a Navy lieutenant, saw a Japanese destroyer sink a U.S. naval vessel, PT-109, and sent two islanders in a dugout canoe to rescue the boat's skipper—Lieutenant John F. Kennedy—and his crew.

When Curran realized that the story of President Kennedy's rescuer had never been told, he hired an Australian writer to do a piece for *Cavalier*. Then Curran and his Managing Editor, Bill Wise, asked the Fawcett brothers to bring Evans to New York—think of the publicity! Tight-fisted and unimaginative, the brothers refused, but an Australian press service said yes. Then, with Curran triumphantly at his side, Evans went to Washington and chatted with President Kennedy.

"A story about that meeting and a photo of Evans and Kennedy at the White House were on the front page of the *New York Daily News*," Wise recalled. "You couldn't ask for more." Oddly, at some point there was also a visit to Yonkers Raceway, near New York, where one of that night's trotting races was named after Evans. "He was a nice, modest man," Wise says. "People jammed around him, asking for autographs. Then he went back to Australia and as far as I know, sank into obscurity."

* * *

A travel agency contacted *True* about a two-week "Bachelor Party Tour" they'd cooked up: roughly forty single men and women would go from New York to the Mediterranean on a luxury liner, visit Rome, Paris, and London, and fly back. Would *True* like to send someone along for free, with a possible article in mind? This expensive tour was to take place over Christmas and New Year's; most *True* editors were married, and wanted to be home then; I volunteered. During the very first shipboard dinner, I began to doubt that I'd be able to produce the hoped-for romantic piece. Most of the women were middle-aged, well-off, husband-hunting widows or divorcées; the men—also middle-aged and well-off—had expected to get laid. Both sexes looked grumpy. However, within a few days, they began to enjoy themselves: the tour was well-run, the sightseeing was interesting, and we ate well. I suspect that some friendships were made.

I shared accommodations with the tour director, a cheerful fellow a few years older. One afternoon in Rome, he staggered into our hotel suite carrying a forty-pound stone slab carved with crude bas relief figures and announced it was a genuine Roman relic—the Italian who'd approached him on the street and sold it to him for many American dollars had said so. "It'll look great in my living room," he added.

I pointed out that if the thing was authentic—which I doubted—it was illegal to take it out of Italy. And how was he going to get it to the U.S.? Under his seat, as carry-on luggage?

When we departed for Paris, he left it in a closet. No doubt, it was soon sold again.

* * *

I'd been at *True* for over two years. I wanted to get away from New York and away from nine-to-five. I'd saved a little money, and had an article assignment from *Cavalier.* I wanted to spend some time in Paris and see if I could support myself by writing.

Before leaving, I went to say goodbye to Ralph Daigh in his comfortable office. Looking dapper, as usual, he listened to my plans and wished me well. Then his eyes brightened. "I love Paris. I get there as often as I can." He pulled a snapshot out of a desk drawer. I knew he had a wife in New York—but here was a pretty young woman, in a nightgown, seated on a balcony, with the Eiffel Tower in the background, demurely sipping her morning *café au lait*. She looked charming.

Ten

PARIS

In the past seven years, I'd gone from Doubleday into the Army, then back to Doubleday, and then to *True*, working steadily, job-to-job, with no real time off. Now, I had no ties, no obligations, no plans beyond a loose itinerary and a project that would bring in some cash. I'd like to say that when I boarded the bus that would take me to the airport in late October '59, my eyes were gleaming and my heart beating fast and my ears ringing with thrilling song, but that would be a lie. In fact, a good part of me felt worried. I was headed ultimately for Paris—where I had no place to live, and knew exactly one person. What was I doing? Was this crazy, going off this way? Would I be back in six months with my tail between my legs?

My first stop was London, to research my magazine assignment. My passport, bearing the pompously convoluted signature of Secretary of State John Foster Dulles, said I mustn't travel to any foreign state "for the purpose of entering the armed forces of such a state" ("Dammit, John Foster," I silently said, "that was *exactly* my purpose!"). Ironically, my assignment took me straight into the embrace of the British military. My subject was "Bluey" Truscott, a Royal Australian Air Force ace who shot down fifteen German planes during the Battle of Britain. At the Air Ministry's Records Division in Whitehall Gardens, I was given a temporary pass and spent a day in the library. The pass was marked THIS MUST BE GIVEN TO THE DOORKEEPER ON LEAVING THE BUILDING; I still have it. I was staying at a cheap hotel, and one weekend travelled to Stratford-on-Avon with Glenn Paxton, a composer my age who had already had a musical produced on Broadway (Bo Goldman, whose father owned a fake Winslow Homer, wrote the book and lyrics). John Sack, the equally young author of a funny travel book, came along with us (he and Jerry Goodman, as Harvard housemates, used to put condoms on their dog's paws on snowy days; in 1966, Sack wrote a famous *Esquire* article about a U.S. Army infantry company in Vietnam). The three of us got along splendidly; I should've taken notes on the brilliant things we said in the car, during dinner, and in the pub after the play.

In New York, John Sainsbury, a genial Londoner and heir to the vast British supermarket chain, had invited me to stay at his splendid Eaton Terrace house. He took me to dinner at his posh London club and showed me around his posh school, Eton, but after two nights I realized that his anti-American houseman, Saul, hated me: when I asked for ice in my Scotch and soda, his lip curled in disdain. John has since been knighted, chiefly for his gifts to the National Gallery. That must've raised Saul's status among his peers, and I'm sure that he's now *truly* insufferable. (Not long after my visit, Anthony Armstrong-Jones lived briefly in John's house to escape the spotlight before his marriage to Princess Margaret; perhaps he had the honor of sleeping in the bed I slept in.)

In Paris, the hotel where I'd stayed in '51 was full, so I wound up in one on the rue Bonaparte. My room was four elevatorless flights up, the toilet was in the hallway, the bathtub was two flights down, and the pay phone was in the lobby—but I was in one of the city's most wonderful neighborhoods. The Boulevard St. Germain was a short walk to the south and the Seine was a short walk to the north; within minutes, I could reach the Café des Deux Magots or Notre Dame. Nowadays, those narrow streets are jam-packed with trendy, expensive shops selling jewelry and handbags and antiques, but then the buildings housed family-run bakeries, grocery stores, cheese shops, and cafés—and, best of all, intimate, inexpensive restaurants. After drinks at a café, you could stroll in, no reservations needed, and for a third of what you'd pay in New York, have a marvelous dinner (I learned to love offal: sweetbreads, brains, and best of all, kidneys). One night, out of curiosity, I asked the lady behind the cash register why almost all French chefs were men. Her eyes lit up with pride. "Because, Monsieur," she said, pointing at the open kitchen door, "It takes great endurance—like my husband!" Sure enough, the man with the toque, flourishing a spatula, was sweating fiercely, and looked indomitable.

The only person I knew in Paris was a cousin, Mary Maverick Lloyd. I called her soon after I got there, and she suggested lunch in a restaurant. Then fifty-two, Mary was slender, brown-haired, and humorous, with a quick laugh and strong opinions ("In France, everyone has a *real face*; not so in America"). She'd been in and out of Paris for years, spoke perfect French, and was now living, she told me vaguely, "in the Fifth Arrondissement—the Latin Quarter" and working hard to promote the cause of world government. I loved being with her and saw her once a month—and later she did me an enormous favor.

People complain that the French, particularly Parisians, are rude; there's a joke that goes, "God found Paris too perfect, so he created the Parisians." My experience was, yes, they were sometimes brusque— like residents of big cities everywhere. Within just a few weeks, I became affectedly, obnoxiously Francophile. I didn't wear a beret, but I drank Pernod and smoked Gauloises. Trying to improve my French, I read French newspapers and magazines. (Some years later, the best-known magazine, *Paris-Match*, ran a long piece of mine about a Paris art forger who'd been caught in New York.) When French people didn't understand my name, I said, "*Comme les pneus*" ("Like the tires") and they got it. I can't say that I "blended into Parisian culture," but few foreigners expect to. For them, that's not important. What matters is, the city is a stunningly beautiful wonderland where they have adventures they wouldn't have elsewhere.

* * *

Today, the patrons at the Deux Magots seem to be mostly camera-toting Japanese, everything costs too much, and if it's crowded, you may be pressured into buying a second drink or leaving. Back then, many actual Parisians visited, the prices were reasonable, and you could nurse a beer for hours. A gorgon with a mustache knitted in the men's room; you had to tip her for the privilege of pissing. In winter, the place was a warm, smoky refuge where patrons thawed with exotic-sounding hot drinks. At the first scent of spring, you sat outdoors, serenaded by taxi horns and muttering motor scooters, and watched the passing show: chic, clever-looking women dressed by the world's greatest couturiers; bearded, would-be filmmakers carrying that day's shots in cans; businessmen carrying briefcases and trying to look important. There was a lot of cheek-kissing. Long-robed Arabs appeared, hawking carpets of the finest possible quality and lowest conceivable price; a tiny woman named Poucette offered to draw your portrait. Next door was the Café Flore, where you could catch a glimpse of Sartre and de Beauvoir; across the Boulevard St. Germain was Brasserie Lipp, serving the world's zestiest choucroute—which I couldn't afford.

Most of the pals I made at the Deux Magots were American. Paul Deutschman, a Paris veteran, wrote articles for American magazines and told funny stories about trying to persuade French café owners to make iced coffee. Richard Gilman, young and good-looking, was on a trip around the world after selling the movie rights to his Hawaii novel, *Diamond Head*. "Whatever country I'm in," he said, "I find dates in ballet companies—I go to the theater and stand at the stage door. The female dancers are lonely because the male dancers are all queer." Gilman had a lively, strong-minded French girlfriend (a painter, not a dancer). A few years later, visiting New York, she told me, "The only handsome people here are the blacks." The motorcycle-riding American painter John Levee had lived in Paris for years, and once pointed with delight at a large outdoor poster announcing a show of his work at a leading gallery, saying, "That's why I live here. They appreciate artists." I went to the gallery opening and to the party afterwards, in a gorgeous apartment overlooking the Seine. Rufino Tamayo—now world-renowned and gray-haired—was there, wearing not a paint-stained smock, but a beautifully cut Savile Row suit. He remembered me, and I remembered not to call him "Mr. Tomato."

* * *

From my hotel, I explored Paris, riding the Metro, then walking—I'd never walked so much. I became one of the city's "flâneurs" (dawdlers) without ever having heard that word. I loved some of the clichés—the roasted-chestnut-sellers, the street-sweepers' twig brooms—but skipped others; I never went up the Eiffel Tower. (Another joke: when the tower was new, some Parisians said they hated it, and went up only because from there they couldn't see it.) At Paris's highest point, Montmartre, I found bad painters working on—and offering for sale—bad paintings of Sacré-Coeur; in Montparnasse, I found heavenly oysters and delicious beer at the cavernous La Coupole. While walking, I came upon the signs of two wars. When Allied Forces reached Paris in August 1944, French Resistance fighters died, helping to oust the Germans; all around the city, plaques bore their names. One hit me hard; at that exact spot on August 22nd, my fourteenth birthday— maybe while I was blowing out the candles on my cake—a young fighter was killed. Now, the war in Algeria was raging, with many casualties there—and some in Paris. Outside police stations and government buildings, cops wearing capes and kepis and carrying machine guns stood behind cement anti-hand–grenade barriers; heavy-booted, garrison-capped men from the CRS ("Compagnie Républicaine de Sécurité," known for their brutality) patrolled in trucks and on foot. Twice, I saw puddles of blood being hosed off sidewalks: Paris's Algerians sometimes knifed each other.

* * *

Bodie Nielsen had urged me to go to Copenhagen— "It's pretty and cheap, and you'll love the people." In November, I made the trip, stopping overnight in Amsterdam and visiting the house where Anne Frank hid. I had no trouble finding it; every Amsterdam resident seemed to know the address. Just as Aunt Frances had five years before, I stretched out my arms in Anne's room and touched the walls on either side, and found it harrowing. (The Hacketts had given generously from their royalties from the play to help restore the site as a memorial.) On the train to the Copenhagen ferry, I had a drink with the extra-friendly Finnish gymnastics team, joyfully returning to Helsinki after defeating the Swiss in Geneva. The ferry carried massive trucks whose massive drivers shouted in the bar. Bodie was right about "cheap": at a comfortable, sixty-room hotel in Copenhagen's quiet, historic center, a room plus breakfast cost $2.10. In the library of the nearby, admission-free students' center—not really a library, but a dormitory: the students slept often and read seldom—I finished the Truscott piece. Every hour, church bells rang; everywhere, there were seagulls overhead. I couldn't speak the language, I knew no one, and no one knew me (total freedom squared). I *did* have the phone number of an agent who'd sold the Danish rights to a short story of mine. With typical Danish hospitality, this attractive, middle-aged, English-speaking lady gave me a delicious dinner in her apartment. The Danes were nuts about American jazz. In a club with wonderful Danish beer and wonderful Stan Getz, I met a pretty, cigar-smoking Danish girl whose bed turned out to be a door on sawhorses. As in Paris, I walked many miles, particularly around the harbor, enjoying miniature frankfurters sold from carts. I may be the only foreigner to visit Copenhagen without going to the Tivoli Gardens. The city was full of aspiring young writers and artists. I went to some exhibits; from an American writer, I heard vicious anti-Americanism: "Three Americans were just hanged in Tunisia for selling salad oil cut with motor oil! Ten thousand people got crippled! Serves the Yankees right!" I said that I read the *Paris Herald Tribune* every day, but hadn't seen that major story. "Well," he replied, emptying his glass, "It happened."

* * *

Back in Paris, I started work on a novel I'd been planning, based on the Bachelor Party Tour I'd taken while at *True*. It was supposed to be funny. I beavered away 'til I had fifty pages, then realized they were no good because, at bottom, I didn't like my characters.

One day, walking on the Right Bank near the Place de la Concorde, I saw a dozen yachts tied up at the quay. On the deck of a sturdy, forty-six-foot ketch called the *Tzu Hang* were its mid-fifties, English-born owners, Miles and Beryl Smeeton, and their cat and dog. The Smeetons invited me on board, and I got involved in their story.

Miles—six feet seven inches tall, with amazingly long legs and a twinkle in his eye even when describing painful events—had been a brigadier in the Indian Army. Before the war, he'd had a fantastic life of polo, pig-sticking, and mountain climbing. Beryl was also wondrously adventurous and had travelled thousands of miles on horseback and on foot and on primitive buses and trains through four continents, always alone. Together, they climbed the Himalayas; for several years, Beryl held the women's altitude record.

In 1946, after Miles had fought heroically in North Africa and Burma (he was called "the quintessential professional soldier"), he and Beryl settled in British Columbia and started farming. In 1955, they bought *Tzu Hang* and, with their cat and their dog, went cruising, covering twenty thousand miles. They island-hopped across the Pacific to Australia, then headed into the fierce seas surrounding Cape Horn. There, during a heavy storm, they were nearly killed. Beryl was alone on deck; looking astern, she saw, as she later wrote, "something incredible—a wave twice as high as the others, an absolutely vertical, seventy-foot, gray-green cliff with white water running down its face." The wave flipped the boat upside down and damaged it heavily, and crushed Beryl's vertebrae, fractured her ribs, and threw her overboard. Miles pulled her back onboard; thirty-eight miserable days later, *Tzu Hang* crept into a Chilean harbor. After eight months of recuperation and rebuilding, they set off again to round the Horn—and another double-decker wave smashed them. They made the second attempt, Beryl wrote, because they were convinced that the first wave had been a freak and, more importantly, "If we *didn't* try again, we would be afraid forever after, and you can't go on cruising if you feel that way."

Beryl and Miles were good-looking, witty, and madly energetic; I admired them enormously, and visited often. Miles was a gifted writer; a British firm had published his book about the Cape Horn experiences, *Once Is Enough*, which made him famous in the yachting world. Beryl was working on an article reflecting her own feelings about life aboard *Tzu Hang* (she wrote that the name was Chinese for "both 'Charity Pleasure Boat' and 'Kept Woman'—take your pick"). Unfortunately, her writing was awkward, and dyslexia produced odd spelling ("holet" for "hotel"). She asked me to help, and we worked together, sometimes on the boat and sometimes in my room. In her diary, Beryl called me a "very nice American," which I guess is a compliment. In the boat's guest book, my signature is just above that of the bestselling author Emily Hahn, who was Beryl's sister-in-law. Beryl and I sent our long article to Willis Wing, hoping—vainly—that he could interest an American magazine. (Beryl *did* sell articles to British magazines and later published *Winter Shoes in Springtime*, a book about her earlier adventures. Miles wrote nine more books, about his soldiering years, cruising, mountaineering, and exploring. The Smeetons have been called "the most accomplished travelling and adventuring couple of the twentieth century.")

The Smeetons were in Paris sort of by accident. Their original goal had been London, but when they got there, they realized that they would have to quarantine their beloved pets. The French were more lenient, so *Tzu Hang*'s masts were taken down to allow passage under the Seine's bridges. The Smeetons' Paris life was extraordinary. They were paying only a small dockage fee to live in the heart of the world's most beautiful city. Their quarters on *Tzu Hang* were comfortable. The galley was small, but Beryl's meals were satisfying. (Once, a visiting couple insisted on getting the recipe for a hastily prepared, delicious curry, and she admitted using two cans of Kit-e-Kat; luckily, I wasn't there that evening.) Their daughter Clio, an art student, visited often from London. Their French friends entertained them exotically: rock-climbing in Fontainebleau, deer hunting with a duke in the Bois de Boulogne. The only drawback, Miles told me with a grin, was "the occasional Algerian corpse." One evening, he found one stuck between the quay and the boat; using a boathook, he sent it downstream just before the dinner guests arrived. Another time, he saved an elegantly dressed woman from suicide. He saw her roll her black suede gloves into a tiny ball, then jump. He pulled her ashore in the dinghy and tried to warm her up. After firemen took her to the hospital, he realized she'd gone off wrapped in the dog's blanket.

* * *

Because of my mediocre French, I'd become friendly with only a few Parisians. Now, I met a gorgeous, young woman, Anne, whose family name included "de la." She invited me to Sunday dinner in the ritzy Sixteenth Arrondissement. This was an honor: very few foreigners were ever included in family occasions. The apartment was grand and Anne's parents were kind; there turned out to be two equally gorgeous younger sisters. As I gazed around, and tasted the marvelous food, I was nearly tongue-tied, and secretly wished I'd been brought up in Paris and had "de la" in *my* name.

Another Eton-type Englishman whom I'd met in New York was now editing picture books for French children; for him, the job was a lark. He hired me to do a translation, saying, "Don't worry about being *accurate*; the pictures tell the story." Then Bob Curran, the editor of *Cavalier*, sent another assignment: a piece on the current status of the guillotine. Curran said he thought one still existed, and there might still be an official guillotiner—what could I find out? That research would've been tough—where would I find written material (which I'd have to read in French)? Talk about luck: I'd recently met a Frenchwoman who'd just researched the exact same subject for an American writer named Geoffrey; for a fee, I could use her translated notes and clippings. Geoffrey objected: he didn't want competition. I pointed out that our pieces would be similar no matter where I got my material— and besides, he had a head start, so he'd be published first. He dropped his objections and I set to work.

Although my hotel bills were small, my income was also small, and my savings were dwindling. It was obvious I couldn't stay in Paris much longer—but then something miraculous happened. Every few weeks, Mary Lloyd had been treating me to lunch in a different restaurant; the food was always delicious, and we were the only Americans there. At lunch in February, she told me she was leaving Paris for several months. Would I like to housesit for her?

Would I!

All along, I'd wondered why Mary never invited me to her house—and now I was introduced to the reason. In those days, ladies didn't live with gentlemen they weren't married to, and for several years, Mary had shared an ancient, narrow, gray-painted dwelling, 55 rue Lacépède, in the Place de la Contrescarpe (near the Pantheon) with Jacques Savary, a middle-aged, solidly built, scholarly looking Frenchman. The two had never married, someone told me, for a sad reason: Savary had a mentally ill wife who was in a sanatorium; if he divorced her, "it would be too much for her."

Jacques Savary was as passionate about world government as Mary was. On the ground floor of 55 rue Lacépède was an office called the Centre Mondialiste, where they wrote articles and ran something called the International Registry of World Citizens. Above the office were three more stories. I was to live on the second, which consisted of the dining room, the kitchen, and a bathroom; a small table would replace the dining table, and a cot would be set up. The two upper stories contained bedrooms, a living room, more WCs, and a bathroom. "Please go upstairs occasionally to see if everything's okay," Mary said, "and, of course, use the bathtub."

The Place de la Contrescarpe was in a working-class neighborhood. For decades, the low rents had attracted needy writers. The poet Paul Verlaine spent his last years haunting Contrescarpe cafés, blotto on absinthe, and died in a squalid hotel on an adjoining street. When he was in his twenties, Ernest Hemingway lived right around the corner. In *The Snows of Kilimanjaro*, he called the Place Contrescarpe "the square":

> There never was another part of Paris that
> I loved like that, the sprawling trees, the
> old white-plastered houses painted brown
> below, the long green of the autobus in
> that round square, the purple flower dye
> upon the paving, the sudden drop down
> the hill of the rue Cardinal Lemoine to
> the river, and the other way the narrow
> crowded world of the rue Mouffetard.

When I moved into Mary's house, the bus still ended its run across Paris in the square beside a homely, metal-roofed rain shelter; the flower sellers still dyed their flowers purple; and the houses all seemed to lean toward the street. Clochards—tramps—slept on hot air grates in the sidewalk. The rue Mouffetard was one of Paris's oldest streets: it followed the path of the Roman road to Lyon. An open-air market was set up there every Saturday, and you could buy everything from rhubarb to babies' teething rings. On my first evening in my new home, I bought a steak in a butcher's shop on Mouffetard. It was tough and tasted funny; the next day I noticed that the shop's sign featured a golden horse's head. The square had shops of every kind, and a couple of cafés. Hemingway said that one, the Café des Amateurs, smelled of "dirty sweat and poverty and drunkenness." He recalled neighbors who,

> when someone lay drunk in the street, moaning and groaning … would open their windows and then the murmur of talk. "Where is the policeman? When you don't want him the bugger is always there. He's sleeping with some concierge" … 'Til someone threw a bucket of water from a window and the moaning stopped. "What's that? Water. Ah, that's intelligent."

There was a small, antiquated heater in my room. To start it, you lit the end of a slender spill of rolled-up newspaper with a match, turned on the gas, and poked the spill inside. Mary urged me to turn it off while I slept—"If the flame goes out, the gas will kill you"—so I often woke up inside a refrigerator. Mary was a chain-smoker, and upstairs there was a blanket pockmarked with burns; I wondered how often *she'd* almost perished in the night. She asked me to answer the office phone if I happened to be nearby when it rang. Once, a husky female voice asked for Mary in flawless French. The caller was Caresse Crosby, the American-born, now-middle-aged poet, publisher, and patron of the arts; she and Mary had become friends in the early 1950s through their interest in peace organizations. Caresse and her rich American husband, Harry (once called a "fascinating, deplorable, charming, and wretched man") founded the Black Sun Press in Paris and brought out works by James Joyce, Ezra Pound, Archibald MacLeish, Hart Crane, and others. In 1929, Harry and his mistress committed suicide together; he evidently saw that as "the supreme affirmation of love."

I was in the office another day when a tanned, fit-looking man in his late thirties dropped by, carrying an enormous knapsack. This was Garry Davis, the well-known, self-described "world citizen" and peace activist who in 1948 pitched a tent on U.N. territory in Paris and renounced his U.S. citizenship. He had since been travelling the globe and giving out "World Passports" (which he'd invented) and sometimes going to jail. He knew Jacques and Mary because he'd helped to found the International Registry of World Citizens in 1949. Before that, he'd been an actor and a B-17 bomber pilot during the war. His crusading made him controversial, even notorious (someone once said about him, "Clearly the line between being an active global citizen, and becoming a crank, is thin"), but his basic ideas made sense to me. We went for a walk; then I made tea.

My room had only one window—but it was huge, with two giant sides that swung inwards, almost reaching the floor. Looking out, you felt you were in the square itself, floating just above people's heads. I watched workmen pedaling home in the evening with their toolboxes strapped to their handlebars, mothers with children stopping at the bakery for baguettes, the glazier who carried windowpanes in a rack on his back, and the quickly striding, demented man in a business suit who bent over every ten feet to pick up imaginary bits of string.

The hard-drinking, chain-smoking clochards didn't seem pathetic, like today's American homeless; the impression was, they *liked* living outdoors. (I was told that a model, no-cost community, featuring food and drink, medical care, and housing with all the amenities, had once been built for hundreds of them in the country, but almost all returned to the excitement of Paris' streets.) Right next to Number 55 was a students' hotel. The end-of-the-line bus stop was in front of it. Before retracing their route, drivers would have a brandy in the Café des Amateurs, then tease the hotel's crazy concierge; more than once, I saw her silence the teasing with a bucketful of water (water-throwing was big in Place de la Contrescarpe). Several residents owned dogs, which they let out to snooze in the sun and sniff trouser cuffs.

I stayed at 55 rue Lacépède the rest of my time in Paris. Leaving New York, I'd heard no thrilling song, and had been concerned: was I doing something stupid? I got the answer when I moved into the Place de la Contrescarpe. I *adored* the house, the square, the neighborhood, my neighbors, the people I met in bistros and shops and on the street. I was at *home*. I'd been lucky to get to Paris at all; now, I felt doubly blessed, and sang (off key) my version of Oscar Hammerstein's great words, "Now here I am in Paris, her heart is warm and gay, I hear the laughter in her heart in every street café."

* * *

Blessed or not, I still needed money, so I kept on with the guillotine piece. In the evenings, filled with a lifting feeling of accomplishment after pounding my typewriter keys, I walked to have dinner with friends. First, I passed the house where Hemingway had worked.

I had no illusions that I would ever produce anything remotely as fine as he and the other Lost Generation writers had, but I was thrilled to be treading in his footsteps. Then I passed the Pantheon, home to the remains of Zola, Dumas, Voltaire, and others. If I wasn't assimilating with the French, at least I was rubbing elbows with some of their greats.

One night, friends took me to a bar called Les Nuages (The Clouds), a hangout of young Parisians and American writers—William Saroyan, Chester Himes, James Jones. The only clouds were cigarette smoke. Someone told me that a momentous question was pressing down on Sayoran: he was having an affair with a middle-aged woman and was also screwing her twenty-ish daughter; was this ethical? The owner of Les Nuages turned out to be Johnny Romero, whose Greenwich Village place I'd visited with George Plimpton. Romero didn't remember me, but I remembered him. He was still doing his finger-in-the-flaming-brandy stunt—except now, the response was "Ooo-la-la!" There were two stories about why he'd moved to Paris. One was that the Mafia had owned the building housing his New York bar, and once the bar became successful they raised his rent outrageously and forced him to buy his supplies—even the sawdust on the floor—from them, and he got sick of that. The other story said that Romero got overly involved with a mobster's daughter. Whatever the truth was, I was told that his problems as a black man among whites were the basis of the 1970 Pulitzer-Prize winning play, *No Place to Be Somebody*, by Charles Gordone, who'd been a waiter at Romero's bar in New York. In the play, the hero—also named Johnny—wasn't just a saloonkeeper, but also a pimp.

* * *

The French girls I met all turned out to have boyfriends—but then there was Susan, a blonde from

Dayton, Ohio, who'd recently been homecoming queen at her college. This was her first visit to Paris. At restaurants, she ordered Coca-Cola; even the stuffiest waiters smiled, because she had such great, All-American beauty. Her parents were going to join her in the summer, to drive around Europe, so her father told her to buy a big, comfortable Mercedes. In the Place de la Contrescarpe, it loomed as massively as one of the buses; the crazy concierge's eyes almost fell out of her head, and thereafter she greeted me with awe in her voice. Before her parents arrived, Susan and I took a long, lovely drive across France and into Germany. In a town whose name I forget, we visited friends of hers. The husband was a dentist in the Army Medical Corps; one afternoon, as a kind of reverse house present, he cleaned Susan's teeth, and mine, for free.

Susan's parents took us to the super-priced Tour D'Argent, and like good tourists, we ate one of the famous numbered ducks; for once, Susan drank wine, not Coca-Cola. She often said, "There's no way I'm spending my life in Dayton, Ohio." In 1969, she shed the Midwest forever when she married dapper, diminutive, Austrian-born Frank Lloyd, the owner of the Marlborough Gallery, the most important, richest art gallery in the world. They had two children and lived in New York, Paris, and the Bahamas. In a 1983 trial centering on his handling of the works of Mark Rothko, a jury found that Lloyd had tampered with the evidence; instead of going to prison, he was ordered to start an art education foundation. He died in 1998. Susan now lives in her three residences; in New York, a chauffeur drives her in a limousine even bigger than the Mercedes.

Frances and Albert came to Paris—staying, as always, at the Ritz—and took me and Susan out to dinner. My sister, Maddy, had married John Noble, a half-English, half-Australian Cambridge graduate, RAF pilot, and skier who worked for Dupont International in Geneva. The Hacketts, Susan, and I went there in a rented car. Albert drove eccentrically—one foot on the accelerator, one on the brake—and Frances carried a compass in her handbag to check our course and, when being shown a hotel room at night, to determine where the sunlight would come from in the morning. In Basel, we had dinner in a restaurant with Anne Frank's father Otto and his second wife. Like him, she was a concentration camp survivor and her arm still bore the number tattooed on it by the Nazis. Otto Frank was dignified and impressive. Predictably, Frances wept while talking with him. As much as she loved and respected Mr. Frank, Frances knew he could be—let's say, frugal. "I won a bet from Albert," she wrote concerning that evening. "Otto Frank had dinner with *us* in his hometown, not we with *him*."

* * *

During my eight months in the Place de la Contrescarpe, I sometimes cooked my own dinner. To simplify things, I usually had a pork chop, cauliflower, and half a baguette, with Algerian red wine from the cooperative store on the rue de Cardinal Lemoine, and different cheeses; their wonderful variety took me on a gastronomic tour of France; I liked the barnyard-smelling ones best. (One of Charles de Gaulle's few funny remarks was, "How can you govern a country which has two hundred and forty-six varieties of cheese?")

Outside my window, camera crews shot movies and TV shows. At the Café des Amateurs (which still smelled, as it had in Hemingway's time, of sweat, poverty, and drunkenness), I was hired as an extra for a Dinah Shore TV Show. The pay wasn't great, but we were promised free drinks. Ms. Shore showed up two hours late, which was good, because the extras were also served supper. After another delay—a member of the band vomited on-camera—Ms. Shore sang endearingly.

Another evening, in a neighborhood bistro, I realized that a woman at a nearby table was staring at me. She was in her sixties and looked almost as dissolute as one of Van Gogh's absinthe-drinkers. Smiling broadly, she lowered one mascaraed eyelid in a wonderfully lubricious wink. I didn't love the lady, but I did love the only-in-Paris openness of the invitation.

Mary Kaplan's brother, Richard, gave me a ride in his classic, gorgeous, 1930s, French-built convertible. It (of course) stalled as we were entering the heavy traffic whirling around the Place de la Concorde, causing other drivers to hit their horns in Gallic fury. Richard was living in the rue de la Pompe, near an ancient fountain fed by an underground stream, where local housewives filled their drinking water bottles (tap water was said to be risky and store-bought water cost money). I sometimes took my empty bottles there, alongside the housewives; when Richard's visiting mother heard that, my phony "Frenchness" amused her.

One of Richard's friends was the well-known Beat poet, Gregory Corso. He'd spent time in jail and was a hip, scowling, dark-haired, wiseguy with a compact build. His friend, the famous, much-loved Allen Ginsberg, often said that Corso was as good a poet as Keats. Normally, Corso—who, at Johnny Romero's New York bar, had once smashed a glass into another man's face—was aggressively outspoken, but during an evening I spent with him in a jazz club, he was giggly and dreamy-eyed. I soon saw why: marijuana. He offered to share his joint. I'd never tried pot, but felt that smoking it in a jazz club with an ex-con Beat poet who was as good as Keats was essential to my Paris experience. I puffed away, and it did nothing for me, and that ended my descent into drug addiction.

* * *

In the Café des Amateurs, an American art student—as I recall, his name was Len—asked if I knew anything about sailing: "Two other guys and I've bought a broken-down Twelve Meter yacht, cheap. Next week, we sail it from Cherbourg to Calais, and we need help. From Calais, we're taking it to England and fixing it up. Then we'll sail it to New Zealand and sell it, and buy a tugboat with the profit, and take the tugboat to Holland. There's a big demand for tugboats there. We'll make a lot of money."

There were several empty beer bottles on Len's table, and the scheme was obviously nutty, but the invitation was genuine—and exciting! Voyaging on historic waters! Viewing Dover's majestic cliffs! Tracking the Spanish Armada!

Len and I drove to Cherbourg, stopping for a great dinner: kidneys in mustard sauce, strawberries with **crème fraîche**. The next day, the yacht's low price was explained: the sixty-foot-long hull screamed for paint; the rigging looked sick; the mast, normally towering on a Twelve Meter, had been drastically shortened. Down below were a diesel engine and three tiny cabins. The two other owners were there. One, Larry, had been elected skipper, and had equipped himself appropriately: a black yachting cap, a Gauloise in an ivory holder, and a young German blonde on his arm.

We took on a seemingly endless supply of Algerian wine, onions, potatoes, and canned mystery meat, then sailed out into the English Channel. Actually, we didn't sail, we drifted—there was almost no wind, and Larry refused to turn on the engine ("fuel's expensive"). Amidst heavy shipping traffic—mostly rusty tramp steamers that looked nothing like the Spanish Armada—we continued to drift northeast up the Channel. Standing watch at night didn't bother me because my berth was an air mattress on top of the painfully lumpy potatoes. During the next three days, the only excitement—much shouting and gesticulating—came when the blonde moved out of Larry's cabin and into Len's. I was pleased: Len was a fine fellow, fully meriting the honor.

The wind—a serious squall—finally hit on the third evening, blowing out the jib. We put up two others, which also split; they'd been burned by being stowed on top of the exhaust pipe. I never spent a wilder night.

The next day brought soft winds and thick fog. We were nearing Calais, but we couldn't see the buoys— nor, of course, Dover's famed cliffs—and had lost our way. We knew we had to round a promontory called Cap Gris-Nez. Was that it—that surf-dashed headland we could occasionally glimpse through the murk? We were arguing loudly about our location—and out of nowhere loomed an enormous motor yacht. A uniformed crewman shouted at us through a megaphone. We couldn't hear him, because Larry was pointing and desperately screaming at him, "*Is that Cap Gris-Nez?*"

The rest of us screamed, too—at Larry: "*He's trying to tell us something! Shut up!*

Larry shut up.

From the powerboat came, "*Is that Cap Gris-Nez?*"

We decided that if *they* thought it might be, and *we* thought it might be, it *was*. Walking through Calais toward the Paris train, my bones ached, and I vowed that I'd never again sleep on potatoes.

* * *

Cavalier sent me an advance copy of the issue containing my piece about Bluey Truscott, the Australian fighter pilot. There was a two-page, full-color illustration showing a Spitfire, with Truscott in the cockpit, raking a German warship with tracer bullets; the caption said, "Unescorted fighter planes weren't supposed to attack destroyers, but Truscott was never one to back away from a fight." I'd given the story a title I thought stirring (and even poetic)—*The Cobber Who Clobbered the Krauts*—but that had been changed to *Lethal Boy Bluey*. I wasn't proud of the article: it was formula writing. I evidently showed the magazine (which I still have) to a female artist: ballpoint drawings of women, one naked and one wearing a vaguely Ancient Egyptian costume, cover the pages, and there's a note in French: "For the night of Dave. A diabolic night, Stella." I can't recall who Stella was, and I doubt that we were anything more than pals, because my reply, also in French, says, "Cherie—a thousand thanks, but when?"

* * *

One night, in Les Nuages, I was introduced to James Jones and his bright, beautiful wife, Gloria. Jones was small, with a big chest and a jutting jaw. He spoke with a Midwestern accent, sometimes referring reverently to Proust, Voltaire, and Stendhal. I'd heard that he occasionally acted like a character in his great World War II novel, *From Here to Eternity*—crazy drinking, barroom battles; once, anger had made him punch a wall until his fist was soaked with blood—and I wondered what sort of man he really was. We talked about my guillotine piece and I told him that although there'd been no state-ordered beheadings in several years, a middle-aged Parisian named André Obrecht had a lightweight, easily assembled "Cigar Cutter" in his garage, and stood ready to transport it overnight anywhere in the country. Obrecht, I said, had a daytime job, and as official executioner received an extra, tax-free $120 a month. He drove an olive-green Renault truck; he kept the guillotine blade in a black box painted red inside. I'd absorbed these macabre details because they would help pay my bills, but Jones seemed fascinated by them—which made me wonder about him even more.

The next day, a note came from Gloria, inviting me to dinner. That was thrilling: this famous couple's friends included literary superstars. I arrived on the dot at their apartment at 10, Quai d'Orléans, on the Île St. Louis. The living room had a miraculous view of the Seine and its barges and bridges. There were three other guests: Scotty MacGregor, an attractive, dark-haired American actress; Johnny Romero, the owner of Les Nuages; and James Baldwin.

James Baldwin was short and soft-spoken; his bulging eyes shone as he focused intently on what others said. Having read *Go Tell It on the Mountain* and *Giovanni's Room*, I felt that, in a way, I'd already met him. Jones made drinks, and the six of us talked. Plainly, Jones' accomplishments hadn't made him feel superior; he seemed genuinely interested in my writing, especially Noël Favrelière's story.

At dinner, a uniformed, live-in couple served us. The young, blonde English wife—I think her name was Dora—offered the dishes she'd prepared; her husband, a disagreeable-looking Indian name Ghosh, filled our wine glasses.

So far, the evening had gone pleasantly—but Johnny Romero evidently thought that having a cook and butler was pretentious; he dropped a remark about "high-class living." And while helping himself to leg of lamb, he teasingly asked Dora something like, "How's a white lady feel about serving black men?"

Dora flushed, finished passing the lamb, and left the room. The rest of us were silent; Jones said mildly, "Hey, Johnny!"

We all resumed talking; after a moment, Dora returned with vegetables—and Romero made another crack about her being a servant.

Again, Dora left. Now, Jones was annoyed: "Johnny, you don't talk to her like that!"

Romero smiled, plainly enjoying the situation; Baldwin said, "Johnny's only joking."

A few minutes later, Dora was back—and Romero wisecracked again.

I remember thinking that now trouble would start. Jones had been drinking; he didn't look drunk, but who knew what might happen?

A lot happened.

Jones told Romero he fuckin' well wasn't going to treat his servants that way. Baldwin said fuckin' Jones didn't understand the feelings of black men and should overlook Romero's teasing. Jones replied that Baldwin knew fuckin' well that he—Jones—*did* understand black men and cared about them. Voices rose, hands gestured, Gloria kept loudly telling everyone to shut up, Scotty and I looked on—

And then a liquid began splashing onto my leg.

Scotty was sitting beside me; refilling her glass, Ghosh had let wine run over the brim, onto the table, then onto me.

Jones yelled, "What're you doin'?"

"She didn't tell me to stop!" Ghosh slammed the bottle down and strode from the room, looking as though he wanted to kill someone.

Jones blamed Romero: "That's because you said that shit to Dora!" There was more back-and-forth about where the Jones' loyalties should be, with their guests or their servants. Jones rang a bell, trying to get someone to mop up the wine; there was no reply, so he went into another room and came back with a shiny little revolver. He checked the cylinder (it was loaded), stuck the gun in his pocket, then, saying that Ghosh and Dora were probably in their rooms above the kitchen, he disappeared.

Okay, this had to be *real trouble*.

After maybe ten minutes, Jones returned, looking pale. He quickly swallowed a drink. Upstairs, he said, he'd found Ghosh with one hand bleeding heavily: he'd taken a carving knife from the kitchen and, showing Dora how he was going to disembowel Jones (whom he'd previously liked, but now hated), he'd stabbed the wall and run his palm up the blade. Jones had helped him stem the bleeding; before leaving for the hospital, Ghosh had told him off.

"He said he hates working here," Jones reported, "and he's read all my books, and I'm a lousy writer. I asked him, 'Who *do* you like, fucking C. P. Snow?' He's heard I want to hunt tigers in India, and he said he's a member of the Thuggee clan, and if I go there, it'll be easy to get in, but hard to get out. I fired him and Dora. They leave tomorrow. That's the end of them."

Well, not quite.

While the women served the rest of the dinner, Jones and Baldwin (Romero had fallen silent) started arguing about who was to blame for the evening's disaster—and all of America's racial problems. Baldwin's thrust continued to be, roughly, "White men can't truly understand the feelings of black men," while Jones' was, "Not all of us are insensitive." I've since read that there was a strong friendship between them: they'd both lived on society's lower rungs, Jones in the Army, Baldwin in Harlem. Also, Baldwin evidently respected Jones as a genuine liberal, and Jones freely criticized Baldwin's work, once advising him to leave the "nigger shit" out of his writing because in telling a story, basic human nature mattered more than race. The closeness showed that evening: firing off curses and obscenities, they attacked one another, even shouted at one another—but without taking offense or losing control. Despite all their noise, it was obvious that, down deep, both were perceptive and compassionate.

We finished dessert, and moved into the living room for coffee. The debate seemed to be subsiding—

But then came the first after-dinner guests.

They were William and Rose Styron. They were good-looking, smart, and urbane; Styron had a judicious, gentlemanly air. He'd had a tiring day, so he stretched out on the floor with his whiskey glass balanced on his stomach. Then someone related what had been going on, which revived the gamey words. Styron, a Southerner, offered his thoughts about black-white relations, which began to calm the debaters—

Then in came two young Americans, Bill and Gretchen. Jones got them drinks; the barracks expletives resumed. Pretty, blonde Gretchen had never heard those words before, or seen one intellectual bouncing a glass on his belly and another—Baldwin— sticking his head around an open bathroom door while urinating, so he could go on talking. After a few minutes, she whispered to Bill, "Take me home!"

"And miss being with three of America's greatest writers? I'll call you a taxi."

Finally, the squabbling ended. More people arrived, and the party lasted pleasantly until some horrendous hour. As I was leaving, I asked Jones if he planned to write about the evening.

"Maybe," he said, "I'll call it 'A Passage to India.'"

A few days later, I ran into Jones on the Boulevard St. Germain. "I saw Ghosh and Dora out the window the next morning," he said, "waiting for a taxi with their luggage. His hand was bandaged, and he had an expensive English umbrella of mine. I started to go get it, but then decided not to."

Several days after that, Jones met Ghosh by chance. Ghosh hadn't found another job, so Jones gave him a hundred dollars—serious money then—and told him,

"You're a crazy person. I feel sorry for you." Shortly after *that*, Jones learned that Interpol had been pursuing Ghosh and Dora for years because they were jewel thieves. They'd recently been arrested in England: while applying for jobs, they'd offered a letter of recommendation from Jones, which they'd forged on stationery they'd stolen from him.

James Jones' gift to Ghosh confirmed my feeling that Jones was kind and caring. Another thought I was left with: the Jones-Baldwin disagreement ended peacefully because they were *too intelligent* to let anger kill their friendship. I know that sounds banal—but don't we ache nowadays for that kind of intelligence?

* * *

Not long after that strange evening, I realized that I couldn't create a career in Paris, and I'd better go home and try to figure out what to do with the rest of my life. I hated to leave, and my strongest thought as I boarded the bus that would take me to the airport was, *these have been the best months of my life*. It didn't matter one iota to Paris that I'd been there, but if an iota can be multiplied five billion times, that's how much being there had meant to me.

EPILOGUE

As far as I know, James Jones never did write about that evening.

Gretchen, the girl who was so horrified by the language, recently told me she couldn't believe she'd been that naïve and wished she'd stuck around.

When I got back to the U.S. in '59, for many months I insisted on salting my conversation with snippets of French ("à bientôt," "comme il faut"); I must've been unbearable.

Not long ago, I discovered that the Place de la Contrescarpe has changed. Buses no longer stop in front of 55 rue Lacépède and a little, tinkling fountain surrounded by sweet-smelling flowers has replaced the homely rain shelter. In Hemingway's day, the nighttime air carried the moans and groans of working-class drunks; now, the square is the evening destination of young, partying Parisians, who emit the ringing of cellphones and the growling of Ferraris. The fetid—and beloved—Café des Amateurs has become an Italian fast-food joint; when I mentioned Hemingway, the owners asked, "Who's he?"

Time marches on, but I don't always keep up. For example, I don't own a computer—and I smile when people say, "I can't leave the house 'til the repairman comes."

The dumbing-down of America in the decades since the fifties has been appalling. I'm probably dumber, too—but not *that* much, I trust. I'm writing these words just days before Barack Obama is to be sworn in as president; finally, after many wasted years, America seems a nation of hope.

I've published other magazine pieces and some books, and have had interesting times and met intriguing people in the process—but I haven't again felt the thrill of that Ft. Bragg telegram.

Hundreds of the people described on these pages have died. I wish I believed in an afterlife; then I could look forward to seeing them again.

SOURCES AND ACKNOWLEDGMENTS

To aid my memory, I consulted the Internet, periodicals, and books. My mother, bless her, seems never to have thrown away a single letter written to her by friends or relations, including my father and me. Through the years, I too accumulated helpful pieces of paper. My father's memories were set down in two oral histories.

I thank Joy Weiner and Adele Bildersee, who made the Dalton School's archives available, and Berrie Moos and James Rugen, who did the same at Loomis. I also thank Beth Golembeske, Karen Corrigan, Patricia Christiansen, Prudence Fallon, and Marjorie Lint, of the Brownell Library in Little Compton, for their work. Shael Colantonio and Jean Biddle's research contributions were invaluable, and I'm grateful to Barry Beckham and his staff for their great efforts. For help of various kinds, I'm grateful to: Anita Duquette, Josephine Humphrey, Don McKinney, Bill Wise, Perdita Finn, Phil Havens, Hilary Woodhouse, Tom Burns, George Adams, Kilty Gilmour, Ann Ripley, Sadja Greenwood, Jerry Goodman, Marilyn Penney, Steve O'Connor, Alan Stamn, Monica Larner, Christine Larner, James McMullan, Buck Henry, Nick Kelley, Dominique

Browning, Madeleine Noble, Frances Hall, Maxwell Huntoon, Beth Payne, Karen Lerner, and Clio Smeeton. If there are factual errors in these pages, I'm the one to blame.

Breinigsville, PA USA
14 October 2009
225839BV00001B/9/P